Praise for
Leadership Vertigo

"*Leadership Vertigo* offers practical and effective tools for avoiding self-deception and empowering those we seek to lead. By internalizing Naseer and Brown's four *C*s of leadership—Community, Competence, Credibility, and Compassion—leaders can work to develop an adaptive leadership approach for the increasingly demanding modern age."

—Douglas R. Conant
Chairman, Kellogg Executive Leadership Institute;
Chairman, Avon Products; Founder and CEO, ConantLeadership;
Former CEO, Campbell Soup Company

"Leadership can be learned but must be continuously refined, requiring personal reflection and focus. All of us search for expertise, but the literary marketplace is flooded with lengthy, complex 'solutions.' *Leadership Vertigo* offers timely learnings in this brutally competitive and complex environment."

—John Loomis
VP and Corporate Officer, General Electric Company (retired)

"*Leadership Vertigo* is a precious gem of a book. Max Brown and Tanveer Naseer explore the timeless truths of what leaders must do to create an engaging and meaningful workplace when the world keeps spinning us off course. Their four fundamentals capture the essential lessons for our times, their compelling examples are from real leaders who have genuinely lived these lessons, and their heartfelt passion grabs hold and won't let go. *Leadership Vertigo* is one of those books you'll read in one sitting, but return to time and again. Enjoy."

—Jim Kouzes
Coauthor of the award-winning and best-selling *The Leadership Challenge*;
Executive Fellow of Leadership,
Leavey School of Business, Santa Clara University

"Community, competence, credibility, and compassion are absolutely essential to great leadership. Thank you so much for writing this book, Max and Tanveer!"

—Chade-Meng Tan
Jolly Good Fellow of Google and
New York Times best-selling author of *Search Inside Yourself*

"Max and Tanveer nailed it! Every leader can get off course, and this is the guide for getting back on track."

—Jamie Naughton
Speaker of the House, Zappos.com, Inc.

"Whether you are a seasoned executive, an aspiring leader-to-be, or a recent college student, *Leadership Vertigo* provides real-life examples of meaningful leadership principles that are applicable on a global basis. Simply put, Max and Tanveer have authored a must read by reinforcing the importance of *EVERY LEADER* earning the right to lead *EVERY DAY*!"

—A. Mark Guthrie
Manager, Global Employee Relations, General Electric Company

"Whether you manage tens of thousands of people or just a few, *Leadership Vertigo* is a must read! S. Max Brown and Tanveer Naseer have written a great book on leadership that contains useful information that is actionable. I like to think of the four *C*s in Community, Competence, Credibility, and Compassion as a four-leaf clover with all the leaves facing inwards toward those we lead and with all the benefits that come from leaders who are firmly grounded!"

—Peter Hart
CEO, Rideau Recognition

"I just finished reading *Leadership Vertigo: Why Even the Best Leaders Go Off Course and How They Can Get Back On Track* by Max Brown and Tanveer Naseer. It is well worth the read if you are looking to improve your leadership skills, help someone else improve their leadership skills, or simply want to make a more meaningful impact in your workplace."

—Lisa Krouse
EVP and Chief HR Officer, FCCI Insurance Group

"Reading *Leadership Vertigo* by Max Brown and Tanveer Naseer is like investing a few hours in intimate collaboration with some of the finest thinkers in business, whose ideas have been linked together, efficiently focused, brilliantly augmented, and then presented by two deep-thinking and broadly experienced observers. The return for making such an investment will find immediate application, plus long-term benefits well exceeding reasonable expectations. This book is a valuable addition to one's bookshelf both as a proximate tutorial and a reminding reference."

—Clark A. Campbell, Ph.D.
Award-winning, best-selling author; CEO, OPPM International;
Chairman of the Board, ProLung Medical Diagnostics

"Max and Tanveer have encapsulated genuine wisdom from many that have 'fruit on their trees' in the orchard we call life. However, after accessing this wisdom, they have developed a system for implementing improvement in our leadership roles. The four *C*s represent to me those principles that anchor the system to reality. I have worked in the healthcare industry for over thirty years. Vertigo and non-alignment of leadership is rampant in our industry. The message that resonates with me could not be more helpful and clear for healthcare today."

—Alan Gleghorn
CEO Christie Clinic

"'Take out your own garbage!' is just one of many insights and examples S. Max Brown and Tanveer Naseer offer up in

Leadership Vertigo, an excellent book on helping leaders achieve the leadership of their dreams."

—Whitney Johnson
Author of *Dare, Dream, Do: Remarkable Things Happen When You Dare to Dream*

"I encourage those who want to be a better leader to read Max and Tanveer's book."

—John Hope Bryant
Author of *Love Leadership*;
Founder, Chairman, and CEO, Operation HOPE, Inc.

"Gratitude is vital for the health and well-being of organizations, but the workplace is often a gratitude-free zone populated by workers and supervisors suffering from 'gratitude deficit disorder.' Brown and Naseer compellingly and humanely demonstrate the potential power of gratitude and related qualities like compassion and humility in building 'leadership landmarks'—those qualities that are foundational for effective leadership. Their insights address the important yet often overlooked knowledge-to-performance gap that we all struggle with in trying to translate what we know we should do into what we actually do. Much more than another recipe for successful leadership, the book's central focus is about leading a better life—and how to regain our balance when we stumble."

—Robert A. Emmons
Editor-in-Chief, *The Journal of Positive Psychology*;
Author of *Thanks!* and *Gratitude Works!*

"Looking for a leadership book that makes a difference? You've found it here. Do yourself and your team a favor and read this book."

—Aaron Skonnard
President and CEO, Pluralsight

LEADERSHIP
VERTIGO

WHY EVEN THE BEST LEADERS GO

OFF COURSE AND HOW THEY

CAN GET BACK ON TRACK

S. MAX BROWN AND TANVEER NASEER

FAMILIUS

Published by Familius LLC, www.familius.com

Familius books are available at special discounts for bulk purchases for sales promotions, family, or corporate use. Special editions, including personalized covers, excerpts of existing books, or books with corporate logos, can be created in large quantities for special needs. For more information, contact Premium Sales at 559-876-2170 or email specialmarkets@familius.com.

Library of Congress Catalog-in-Publication Data
2014948925
pISBN 978-1-939629-30-2
eISBN 978-1-939629-86-9
Printed in the United States of America

Edited by Steve Mette
Cover design by David Miles
Book design by Kurt Wahlner

10 9 8 7 6 5 4 3 2 1

First Edition

DEDICATION

To parents, who both lead by example.

To Sally, my best friend and eternal companion.

To AnLi and Drew, who teach me with their questions and inspire me with their compassion and commitment to serve others.

—S. Max Brown

To my wife, Andrée, and my daughters Alya, Malaika, and Zafina, who are not only my inspiration, but the reason why I aspire to be more. Thank you for helping me stay the course to my dreams.

—Tanveer Naseer

And to all those who lift, lead, and serve.

CONTENTS

FOREWORD

Perhaps the most misunderstood, ambiguous, or diversely understood term in the English dictionary is *leadership*. There are as many definitions of this term as there are its seekers. I have often been asked in interviews, meetings, conferences, and even in airport lounges to define leadership and identify a roadmap to achieving it. I don't think I've ever aced the answer to date! I actually don't even know whether there is an all-encompassing, congruous answer possible to the question. I have therefore always approached leadership as a set of beliefs and actions that—when woven together with great passion, intensity, and integrity—can create a picture or persona so compelling that it would defy all definitions.

These beliefs and actions are my cue cards to identify current and potential leaders. S. Max Brown and Tanveer Naseer have added one very important card in this stack with this book. How managers handle leadership vertigo and constantly correct their course to stay on track is indeed a very valuable idea contributing to our understanding of the human ability to lead.

Both Max and Tanveer are accomplished coaches of enterprise excellence and leadership. Over the years they have enlightened us regarding the moral sensitivity, creativity, and components of the art called leadership. With this book they introduce a concept that promises to tremendously aid leaders struggling to navigate through the uncertainties of today's complex business environment.

I have personally experienced leadership vertigo at many moments in my life. One which I talked about in detail in my book *Employees First, Customers Second* was back in 2005 when I took over the helm of HCL Technologies, a $5 billion global IT services company. I found the company in the throes of what I can now describe as "leadership vertigo." Even though we were expanding at a decent rate, we were growing slower than our rivals and steadily losing market share, mindshare, and talent share. But leadership vertigo was misleading us, telling us that everything was okay when it actually was not.

What would be the right response in such a situation? Do we play safe? Or take the plunge into the unknown? It's like finding yourself on the ledge of a building on fire. In that moment you have only two choices: either wait to be rescued, or decide to take matters into your own hands and leap to safety.

At HCL we decided to take the leap of faith, and what happened thereafter is, as they say, history: we were able to transform our company by increasing its revenues and market cap by six times in just seven years.

Reading this book, I realized just how closely intertwined its leadership principles model was to the transformation journey we chose at HCL. We turned around our company from its state of vertigo to a leadership position by following four stages of change which closely reflect the four pillars—Build Community, Develop Competence, Earn Credibility, and Cultivate Compassion—that Max and Tanveer have so lucidly explained in this book.

In this book we find many such similar examples of leaders and companies who have found themselves on the crossroads and leaned on the tenets of Build Community, Develop Comtetence, Earn Credibility, and Cultivate Compassion to create a sustainable turnaround. And, believe me, such case-studies are a rarity in the world today. My research has shown that only one percent of leadership aspirants actually go on to become a CEO of a large company or lead a successful start-up or takethe helm in their chosen fields! Ninety percent of people are not able to get anywhere close to their aspirations and ambitions. I am sure this data is no different for companies. That's right—all of us as individuals and as companies can go off course at some point in our lives. That is the truth of life. But how we can get back on track is the million-dollar question.

Max and Tanveer answer that question in this easy-to-read, richly anecdotal account. It is a practical guide for individuals who wish to be among the one percent who achieve their dreams by staying on course in their leadership journey. It is, in fact, a valuable read for every manager who aspires to become a powerful and influential leader in his or her organization. As the authors have so rightly argued, "*The truth about leadership in today's organizations is that it's no longer a way of commanding; it's a way of being.*"

I couldn't agree more.

—Vineet Nayar, author of *Employees First, Customers Second: Turning Conventional Management Wisdom Upside Down*; former CEO, HCL Technologies; founder, Sampark Foundation

CHAPTER ONE

UNDERSTANDING

LEADERSHIP VERTIGO AND

THE IMPACT IT HAS ON

OUR ABILITY TO LEAD

Gallup research has found that the top 25 percent of teams—the best managed—versus the bottom 25 percent in any workplace—the worst managed—have nearly 50 percent fewer accidents and have 41 percent fewer quality defects. . . . Gallup research also shows that these managers from hell are creating active disengagement costing the U.S. an estimated $450 billion to $550 billion annually.

If your company reflects the average in the U.S., just imagine what poor management and disengagement are costing your bottom line.

—Jim Clifton, Gallup Chairman and CEO[1]

The Realities Today's Leaders Face

There's no question that today's leaders face not only bigger challenges, but greater uncertainties in today's complex and interconnected global economy. We've experienced technological changes that have improved our ability to promote collaboration, innovation, and creativity across multi-disciplinary teams. We've also witnessed a growing requirement to change not only how we lead our organizations, but also how we select and groom future leaders in our organizations.

Indeed, the shift from the Industrial Age's command-and-control style of leadership to the current knowledge-based economy's more people-oriented and inclusive leadership approach has certainly upended many of the so-called best practices of years past.

Thankfully, the last few decades have seen a wealth of studies, books, presentations, and training workshops on how we can improve the way we lead our organizations, showing us how we can motivate and empower our employees to bring out the best in them and channel our discretionary efforts towards a shared purpose.

Unfortunately, as the quote from Gallup Chairman and CEO Jim Clifton points out, there's clearly a sizeable gap present in many of today's workplaces between what we know we should be doing to improve employee productivity, engagement, and retention, and what we're actually accomplishing through our actions and words.

Of course, when we read these reports reminding us of the persistent low levels of employee engagement, the high turnover rates, and the decline in overall productivity, we may assume that this is a remnant of the massive downsizing measures done in the 1980s to "streamline" processes and improve organizational efficiency.

Or that it's simply reflective of the fallout from the Great Recession that hit many industries and countries thanks to the increasing interdependency found in today's global economy.

Or that it's indicative of the increasing workloads leaders now have to manage, along with the increasing number of communication channels they now have to stay on top of to establish accessibility and transparency for those they lead.

While all of these are certainly factors behind the current issues plaguing so many of today's organizations, we have to be honest in recognizing that these outcomes are also reflective of our leadership shortcomings.

As pointed out in the Towers Watson 2012 Global Workforce Study, the role of leaders in an organization "has shifted from being a technical expert [who] directs the work of employees to more of a leader who can motivate and coach [his or her] subordinates. Indeed, many employees have high expectations of the managers as 'people managers' rather than task managers."[2]

When we look at some of the organizations that are currently thriving in today's global economy despite these various issues, it's clear that their leaders have found a way to be more attuned to this shift from technical expert to motivational coach, setting the stage for their organizations to be more adaptive and innovative in how they respond to the various changes in demands and needs of those they serve.

Of course, when we examine these successful organizations, we sometimes dismiss their achievements of high employee morale, low employee turnover rates, and year-after-year profitability as idiosyncratic or reflective of an unusual culture which happens to thrive under the current economic conditions.

And yet, going back to all those studies and leadership books, we find that what these organizations are doing is not unique or unreproducible. Rather, it comes down to the simple truth that their leaders have found a way to consistently deploy the strategies and tactics that allow them to do a better job serving those under their care.

So how come we're not able to do the same? If we're all facing the same issues of having fewer resources and less time to do things, if we're all pressured by increasing demands from our employees for our time and attention, why is it that some of us are able to meet these expectations while the rest of us are missing the mark?

It's not because some leaders care more than others or are more committed. Indeed, the reason there are so many books detailing the success stories of these thriving organizations—not to mention the numerous biographies of the leaders who helm these successful organizations—is because *we are committed to doing better*; we want to achieve the level of success that the leaders and organizations we hold in high esteem have attained.

So what, then, is behind this disconnect between what we know we should be delivering to our employees and what we're actually delivering?

Based on our collective experiences working with leaders from various organizations across a range of industries and sizes, we've come to recognize that the gap that exists between what we know we should be doing and what we actually are doing is due to a subconscious phenomenon which gives rise to false signals in our daily perceptions—false signals that cause us to shift off course from what we ultimately want to achieve.

We refer to this phenomenon as *leadership vertigo*. It's this subtle phenomenon that leads to the dissonance seen in so many workplaces today resulting in lower rates of engagement, productivity, and retention.

But, before we discuss further what exactly leadership vertigo is and how we can better manage those moments when we suffer bouts of this phenomenon, let's first look at what *vertigo* traditionally means.

What is Vertigo?

When we think of vertigo, a common image that comes to mind is that famous scene from the Alfred Hitchcock film *Vertigo* shot from the perspective of James Stewart's character. As he glances over the staircase railing down to the floor below, we see the stairwell suddenly pulling away, creating the illusion that the floor is moving even though we're standing still.

Although it made for a dramatic visual effect, the reality is that vertigo is not usually that obvious, nor does it always impair our ability to act or move. As ear, nose, and throat surgeon James W. Fairley describes it, vertigo is "a particular form of dizziness or giddiness. Rather than just feeling faint or lightheaded, it is an illusion of motion. Vertigo results when the brain believes the false signal and acts accordingly."

In other words, the real danger with vertigo is not an obvious distortion of reality like that which Stewart's character suffers when he looks down the staircase and sees it expanding away from him. Rather, as Fairley points out, the danger from vertigo arises when our brain sends out false signals that inform us we're moving in a certain direction when in reality we're not.

It was this kind of spatial disorientation which investigators concluded was behind the crash of John F. Kennedy Jr.'s plane. He was convinced that he was flying his plane in a level direction, even though his gauges were telling him that he was headed on a much sharper downward angle towards the ocean floor.[3]

Although one might expect vertigo to be an affliction that only new or inexperienced pilots suffer from, it's a common risk for pilots and is a costly issue for many aviation organizations. The United States military alone spends $1 million a day to cover losses incurred as a result of plane crashes caused by pilots suffering from vertigo.[4]

So, while Hitchcock might have created a visually dramatic and memorable impression of how vertigo impaired Stewart's character in his film, vertigo is a lot harder to recognize than we might think.

ONE PILOT'S FIRST-HAND EXPERIENCE WITH VERTIGO

"Vertigo, or spatial disorientation, is a tough concept to those who've never experienced it. It's not the extreme dizziness you get when you spin around with your forehead on a mop handle and then try to walk a straight line. Rather, it's the more subtle form that can be the most profound danger to new instrument pilots.

"I can remember, during primary training hood work, the sensation of feeling my inner ear screaming I was straight and level. Meanwhile my eyeballs relayed the irrefutable evidence to my brain that my inner ear and the seat of my pants were wrong.

"I banked the few degrees to the right to level the horizon. Immediately, my inner ear told me I was a fool. Anyone could tell that I was now in a right bank. But as I fought off the tendency to bank back to the left (with some 'encouragement' from the instructor), the ear fluids settled down. Eventually, all my body parts agreed that we had straightened up and were flying right." —Mark Phelps[5]

What is Leadership Vertigo?

Perception is real even when it is not reality.

—Edward de Bono, physician, author,
and originator of the term *lateral thinking*

We can see how vertigo presents a risk to pilots, but how does vertigo pose an issue for leaders? What are the concerns and problems that we can attribute to an on-the-ground affliction of vertigo? In order to answer that question, let's first start with a definition of what we are referring to when we talk about leadership vertigo:

> Leadership vertigo refers to false signals being sent by our brain asserting that everything is moving along as it should when it's not.

While all of us are susceptible to experiencing this distortion in our perception, as a leader, the risk is greater because it's *your* vision and guidance which serves to inform your team as to whether things are going well or not. If you are suffering from leadership vertigo, your condition will impact how your employees view their contributions and roles within your team and, ultimately, their performance.

Granted, for most leaders, this doesn't translate into a life or death scenario as it does for the aviation industry. However, the consequences of suffering from leadership vertigo are real and

can cost your organization millions, if not billions, of dollars—
Lehman Brothers, Kodak, Enron, and Borders bookstores are
just a few examples of this.

For decades, leadership theories have told us that we need to
get fear out of the workplace and to no longer operate purely
from the vantage point of positional authority. These theories
contend that the key to success in today's global economy is
encouraging innovation and collaboration in our workforce by
empowering those we lead. As leaders, we intuitively understand and appreciate the benefits these measures will bring to
our team. And yet, we still struggle to make these changes a
sustainable reality.

The problem we face is not a lack of knowledge of what is
needed to create the kind of workplaces we admire and attempt
to emulate. Rather, it's the phenomenon of leadership vertigo
which distorts our perception of the realities our employees
face in our workplace.

Leadership vertigo sends us false signals assuring us that we
are applying proven leadership theories and concepts properly.
Consequently, problems that arise may give us the miscon-
ception that these approaches don't work in the "real world"
or, at the least, under the unique conditions found in our own
organizations.

A good example of this is when we treat our employees to
lunch only to hear them griping later about the time spent on
that lunch that could've been spent working. Or when recognition given to a team fails to elicit the kind of emotional or

motivational response we were counting on. Or when a leader falsely believes that their attempts to genuinely connect with the team are actually working. Or when we're confused when the mission, vision, and value statements that are plastered all over the organization are largely ignored or viewed with cynicism. Interestingly, we often find that leaders believe that the engagement and employee satisfaction scores are typically much higher than the employee's actual scores.

These are common scenarios that we've all likely experienced.

In this book, we don't want to focus on what you're doing wrong, but on how you can become better at leading your employees by reading the signals around you correctly and making the appropriate adjustments to help you stay on course with what you want to accomplish through your leadership.

The simple truth is that all of us will be affected by leadership vertigo; none of us are immune. As such, the question then becomes: What are we going to do about it? How do we make certain that we have the awareness and understanding we need to ensure that our leadership remains on course?

Four Leadership Principles to Address Leadership Vertigo

Self-deception actually determines one's experience in every aspect of life. Self-deception is like this. It blinds us to the true cause of problems, and once blind, all the "solutions" we can think of will actually make matters worse. That's why self-deception is so central to leadership—because leadership is about making matters better. To the extent we are self-deceived, our leadership is undermined at every turn.

—From *Leadership and Self Deception:
Getting Out of the Box* by The Arbinger Institute

In our section discussing vertigo, we shared with you the story of one pilot's first-hand experience with vertigo and that the reason he was able to overcome it was because he had a coach—in this case, his instructor—who was able to help him *recognize* that his mind and body's perception was wrong so he could make the necessary correction and fly level again.

Now that we have an understanding of what leadership vertigo is—of how we can be deceived by false signals sent from our brain—how do we learn to recognize when we are suffering from a bout of leadership vertigo?

We've developed a model using four leadership principles that can help you to assess, manage, respond to, and, at best, avoid instances of leadership vertigo:

- **Leadership Principle # 1—Build Community**
  An environment where people want to give their best requires a sense of belonging; a sense of community. This all begins with respect and recognition. Effective leaders celebrate when others succeed.

- **Leadership Principle #2—Develop Competence**
  Your energy level and emotions are contagious. The way you relate to others directly impacts results. Your team members will take their cues from the energy and attitude you bring to the table.

- **Leadership Principle #3—Earn Credibility**
  Credibility requires trust. Authenticity and self-awareness are paramount to establishing that trust. Too many leadership "skills" are merely techniques that are perceived as gimmicks by employees because they aren't real.

- **Leadership Principle #4—Cultivate Compassion**
  Compassion requires courage and vulnerability to listen, understand, and act. Wise leaders learn about others by asking questions. Serving others with genuine concern for their well-being creates meaning.

The fact is that our employees need to know that we're providing them with the right conditions and opportunities to not just be successful, but to grow and evolve as well.

There's a connection between how our actions and words are perceived and our success as leaders. That's why we need to develop a strong, clear sense of how it feels to work with us if our employees are to believe in us and what we stand for.

To this end, we need to create a feeling of community, of being a part of something bigger than a collection of individuals. We need to consistently respond with an inquisitive mind, actively listening to our employees to learn from their experiences so that we can encourage them to share their creativity and insights. This is especially true when you are dealing with mistakes and failures. We also need to make sure that our employees see the authenticity behind our words and actions so that they will trust the compassion we exhibit in light of the challenges or obstacles they face.

It's not enough to ask ourselves if we have the right people on the bus. We also have to ask ourselves what actions and behaviors we're exhibiting that might explain why our employees are not performing to the best of their ability.

In other words, your employees will be more willing to support you because they believe and understand that you're not simply looking out for yourself, but that you're driven to create work that is meaningful, that creates a sense of purpose and value, not just for you, but for all concerned.

Putting all this together doesn't mean you won't experience bad days or face situations where things don't go as planned. But when these four leadership principles are consistently put to use, your employees will see and understand that you take pride in their growth and success, and that will help make you a more successful leader.

Over the course of this book, we'll examine each of these principles and how they can help us manage leadership vertigo by asking ourselves the following questions:

- **Build Community:**
  Do people feel like they belong?
  What am I really communicating to my employees?

- **Develop Competence:**
  Why does the way I feel matter?
  How does my energy level and emotions impact the people around me?

- **Earn Credibility:**
  What is it like to work with me?
  Do people believe in me?

- **Cultivate Compassion:**
  How am I helping my employees to do their best work?
  How am I able to help them grow?

While we certainly should rely on trusted advisors and input from our employees to help us better understand what our own answers would be to these questions, it's important that we develop a fine-tuned sense of self-awareness for how our actions and words align with the image we hold of ourselves as leaders.

That's where these leadership principles will come in handy.

What We Want You to Take Away From This Book

We don't want you to think of these four leadership principles as a toolbox that you pull out only when you notice things going awry. Rather, we suggest inculcating these principles into your everyday style until they become a part of the nature of how you lead. We hope this book will help you become mindful of how you appear to your employees, of how you're connecting with those you lead, and what you're communicating through your actions and words on any given day.

To be clear, we're not saying that these leadership principles are a silver bullet. Instead, we want you to think of them as a way to guide you to a powerful way of being. This is important because the truth about leadership in today's organizations is that it's no longer a way of commanding; it's a way of being.

CHAPTER TWO

LEADERSHIP PRINCIPLE #1:

BUILD COMMUNITY

Now, more than ever, a brand or company is judged not by what it says, or even what it sells, but by what it believes. Its actions are a direct reflection of its credo. As the role of communities grows, the vital element that will bind groups is their credo. Tribal in nature, the credo is a glue that holds communities together; the means through which you connect with these groups will not be any doorway other than the value system they hold dear. Ignite, share, and link genuinely to these values, and the people who hold them will follow you.

—From *The Hidden Agenda: A Proven Way to Win Business and Create a Following* by Kevin Allen

We're going to start off our examination of how we can manage leadership vertigo by looking outward from the vantage point where most leaders prefer spending their time—the one where we take time to rise above our daily tasks and demands so we can focus on how to achieve the long term vision we have for our organization.

Of course, the reality is that most leaders are spending less and less time on this important task because of the increasing demands for their time and attention.

When we are able to spend time reflecting on where our organization is, defining where we need it to be, and planning how to get there, it's important that we are mindful of how we're connecting these ideas and plans with the daily realities of our employees.

To that end, let's discuss the first leadership principle, Build Community. Granted, any organization, for all intents and purposes, is a community as it is a group of people coming together to achieve a common goal or outcome. But unfortunately, in many organizations employees don't see the connection between what matters to them and what matters to the organization, as those things which allow them to derive a sense of meaning and purpose in their lives often do not line up with the shared purpose or day-to-day activities of the organization.

As you know, many people—employees and leaders—struggle to attain a work-life balance because these two aspects of their lives are in conflict instead of being in concert with one another.

This is why one of the top priorities of today's successful leaders is to help employees feel a sense of purpose in what they do, as well as feel like valued members of the organization. In our discussion of this leadership principle, we're going to look at helping you answer the following two questions in terms of how you lead your team and organization:

• Do people feel like they belong?
• What am I really communicating to my employees?

As we'll see over the course of this chapter, by finding the answers to these questions, you'll be able to avoid, or at least take the edge off, many instances of leadership vertigo by ensuring that you're providing a personal connection for each of your team members between what they do and the vision that defines your organization.

Understanding the Importance of Community

You need to bring together people with shared values and a desire to be part of something bigger than themselves.

—Tony Hsieh, Zappos CEO

When we think about community, for most of us what comes to mind is the neighborhood or city where we live and, at times, our country. But what about our organization? How many of us actually view our workplace as being a community where we share a common identity and purpose with all those around us?

Certainly, in today's complex and competitive global market, it's critical to an organization's success that all of its employees share a common goal or shared purpose around which all can rally behind when pressing ahead despite whatever challenges or obstacles they might face.

Fostering a sense of community in our organization helps ensure that our employees derive a sense of shared ownership in our collective efforts. This "buy-in" makes it easier to get employees to commit their discretionary effort to our shared purpose because they've made our organization's vision their own.

So how can you foster a sense of community within your team and organizations? More important, how can you ensure that this shared sense of purpose remains a focal point of your organization's efforts in the face of seemingly continual change and flux, conditions which can exacerbate the frequency at which we experience leadership vertigo?

Let's explore two key elements to this leadership principle—those of respect and recognition—by sharing the stories of two successful leaders who, through the most simple of actions, have helped to foster and sustain a powerful sense of community within their organizations. Through their examples, we'll share insights and lessons on how engendering a sense of community will help you sidestep bouts of leadership vertigo.

What Does Respect Have to Do with Community?

You have to make sure you never confuse the hierarchy that you need for managing complexity with the respect that people deserve. Because that's where a lot of organizations go off track, confusing respect and hierarchy, and thinking that low on hierarchy means low respect; high on the hierarchy means high respect. So hierarchy is a necessary evil of managing complexity, but it in no way has anything to do with respect that is owed an individual.

—Mark B. Templeton, president and CEO, Citrix

Imagine what it would be like to be given the responsibility to turn around the fortunes of a unionized manufacturing plant—one where you not only had to deal with falling employee morale, but with increasing pressure from foreign competitors who are not only able to make the same product for less, but who can make more units per day.

Would you be able to guide this team to increase its product output and reduce its operating costs by tens of thousands of dollars per day without laying off employees or outsourcing work? What's more, could you accomplish this by fostering a sense of community among your employees?

Sounds unrealistic? Well, then you haven't met Billy Ray Taylor.

From 2010 to 2012, Billy served as plant manager for the Goodyear Tire and Rubber Company in Fayetteville, North

Carolina, and, under his guidance, the plant not only increased its production of tires from 31,000 tires a day to over 38,000 tires a day, but his plant also reduced its operating costs by $70,000 a day. In addition, Billy and his employees managed to reduce their unit cost per tire from $30 down to $27, creating a savings of $35 million to the company's bottom line.[1]

It's not hard to see why Billy was recently promoted to director of commercial manufacturing for all of North America in the hopes that he can help other Goodyear plant managers accomplish a similar feat at their factories.

It's easy to dismiss Billy's accomplishment as a representation of his unique leadership talent and abilities. However, a closer look at his story reveals how the leadership principle Build Community can help all leaders to ensure they are staying on course in serving those under their care.

When Billy was given the opportunity to turn around the performance of this tire plant, one of the first objectives he had was to get the almost 3,000 hourly workers to stop seeing themselves as simply plant employees. Instead, he wanted them to view themselves as owners who had a vested interest in seeing their collective efforts succeed.

To accomplish this, Billy knew he had to focus on the relationship he had with all of his employees by consistently demonstrating how much he valued their contributions.

In the following series of stories, we'll see how Billy went about creating a sense of belonging and shared purpose within his team, not through words or grand plans, but through the most simple of actions; actions that demonstrated the level of respect and care he had for those under his leadership.

Taking Out Your Own Garbage to Engender Camaraderie

One day as Billy was doing his regular tour of the facility, he stopped in to check out the facility's laboratory. As he looked around, he noticed there was some oil spilled on the floor, the trash cans were overflowing, and several of the floor tiles were cracked or broken. When he asked around to find out why the lab employees were allowed to work under such conditions, all he got were some vague answers and shoulder shrugs.

It soon became clear to Billy that for the lab employees this was simply "the way things are done around here." And while it may have seemed like a trivial matter, Billy knew that allowing such conditions to continue would speak far louder about how these employees were viewed than anything he said about their work or their performance.

As such, Billy went to the facility's cleaning crew and told them that he didn't want his office to be cleaned until the laboratory was cleaned to his personal satisfaction. And he let everyone in the plant know that he didn't want his office cleaned until the situation in the laboratory was improved.

The message Billy wanted to send out to his employees was clear: "If they can work in this type of environment, so can I."[2]

To prove how serious he was, Billy took it upon himself to empty his own trash and vacuum the floor of his office, sometimes in plain view of his employees. Although he never made a big deal of doing these chores, it nonetheless had a powerful impact on his employees.

In fact, not only did Billy's actions result in the facility's laboratory being completely revamped, but the improvements ignited the laboratory employees' drive to share their insights on what else could be improved in the plant, an outcome that led the team to create new continuous improvement processes that saved the plant $144,000 in expenses.[3]

How Clean Bathrooms Can Flatten Your Organizational Playing Field

Sympathy, empathy, looking for similarities, communication—that's all important, but taking action is also critical to effectively relate to others. Pontificating and discussing are best balanced by working with others. Leaders make a powerful statement when they roll up their sleeves and dive in to help out in a situation.

—From *Leading with Humility* by Rob Nielsen,
Jennifer A. Marrone, and Holly S. Ferraro,

Of course, being a tire manufacturing plant, it's natural for other places in this facility to get grimy and messy over time. In fact, not long after the incident with the facility's laboratory, some of the plant workers approached Billy about the dismal conditions in the bathrooms.

After seeing how filthy the bathroom sinks were, Billy went off to see the cleaning crew, but not to find out who was responsible for these bathrooms not being properly cleaned. Rather, Billy asked the cleaning crew where he could get some cleaning supplies and gloves.

Seeing the confused looks on the faces of the cleaning crew, Billy explained to them that he had received complaints about the bathrooms and so, he was going to clean the bathroom sinks. Naturally, the cleaning crew insisted that they would do it, but Billy told them he wanted to do it himself "because I want you to see how important it is to me."[4]

Billy realized that in order to create a respectful environment for his employees, he needed to show them that he would never ask them to do something he wouldn't be willing to do himself.

The idea that a plant manager would take time out of his busy day to clean dirty bathrooms just to prove a point might sound odd to most of us. However, for the people Billy served, his actions became something that they came to respect him for. They began to realize that Billy never hesitated to shake their grease-covered hands as he walked the plant floor because he cared more about being able to connect with those he lead than keeping his hands clean.

Though such actions, Billy was able to reinforce the message he wanted to communicate and instill in his team—that he wanted his employees to see themselves not as just hourly workers, but as members of a community that was driven to accomplish a shared goal.

Of course, while Billy wanted his employees to understand how much he respected and valued their contributions, the real test of whether his tactics would make any difference depended on whether it impacted the way his employees viewed themselves in terms of their roles and contributions.

Transforming Hourly Workers into Entrepreneurial "Plant Owners"

There is no power for change greater than a community discovering what it cares about.

—From *Turning to One Another: Simple Conversations to Restore Hope to the Future* by Meg Wheatley

As Billy left a morning meeting at the plant, he was approached by one of his employees who told him that he needed to show Billy "something that was eroding profits." The employee took Billy to a gondola where there were pipe fittings, ball rings, and other parts that were being thrown out because their plant had no more use for them.

His employee suggested that while their plant didn't need these parts, one of the company's sister plants could certainly benefit from using them. As a result of this employee's efforts, the company saved $27,000 recycling these parts instead of buying new ones for the other plants. [5]

Billy knew that the only reason this employee had taken the time to report this was because he didn't see himself as being just a plant worker. Instead, this employee viewed himself as a plant owner who had a vested interest in making sure the plant did its part to help the company operate effectively, both cost-wise and production-wise.

As Billy points out, although this employee was an hourly worker, "he had to have the confidence that he was the plant manager, that he could bring that to me [and] not say, 'I'm just an operator, it doesn't matter what I say.'" [6]

Billy had been able to demonstrate to his employees that they *mattered*; that they deserved to be treated as people and not as resources. For Billy, his employees were fellow members of a community, a community that ensured their collective success.

Building Something Bigger into What We Do

When you were made a leader you weren't given a crown, you were given the responsibility to bring out the best in others.

—From *Winning* by Jack Welch

If Billy's efforts to communicate how much he respected his employees and valued their contributions could inspire hourly plant workers to demonstrate such a vested interest in how the plant as a whole operates, imagine what could be accomplished using a similar approach in your organization.

Billy was able to foster a sense of community by reminding his employees that their contributions impact their collective ability to succeed and thrive. By exemplifying how his own actions influenced their perception of his role, Billy broadened their perspective to take into account the impact their own actions have on the plant. Billy was able to help his employees develop a greater sense of purpose and how they can contribute in a meaningful fashion to the organization as a whole.

Looking at Billy's leadership example should encourage us to ponder whether we're engendering a sense of community in our organization. Ask yourself, do your employees feel the sense of belonging that Billy's hourly workers did?

COMMUNITY IN ACTION

An MIT-Harvard study found that employees who sat at lunch tables for ten to twelve people had a higher performance level than those who sat at tables for four. This was due to the fact that the former group had a bigger network from which they could get information as well as share ideas and possible solutions.[7]

By relying on this leadership principle to guide and monitor our efforts, we can ensure that we're fostering a sense of shared ownership in our employees, something which Billy's leadership example demonstrates is critical to encouraging our employees to move beyond succeeding on an individual level, towards collaborating and enabling those around them to collectively succeed in their shared goals.

Shared Purpose as an Anchor

Of course, as we've seen, this sense of community has to be anchored to something—it needs to be tied to a vital element or credo, a shared purpose or cause, for it to truly matter to your employees and to those your organization serves.

In most organizations, it's common to find employees who are simply going through the motions, fulfilling only the obligations or responsibilities as defined by their role or function within their team. Often times, we assume the problem lies with our employees, either due to an inherent lack of drive or because we have the wrong people on the bus.

However, the real problem often comes down to what we foster and communicate through our leadership. Do our actions and words engender a sense of belonging? A commonality in our collective efforts among those we lead? Or do we simply treat our employees as task-oriented workers whose sole function is to fulfill their part of a larger process?

Certainly, Billy could have taken that approach given that he was working with hourly workers. However, Billy understood that it was a lack of respect for who these employees were as whole individuals, a lack of connectedness to each other, and a lack of understanding of what each contributed to the organization that had left this plant in such a poor functioning state.

By leading from a position of respect for his employees and a commitment to engender a sense of ownership through what they contribute, Billy not only created a sense of community and shared purpose, but he gained his employees' help in creating a competitive and financially successful manufacturing plant.

Concentrating on how to build this leadership principle into your organization is important when you spend time planning, assessing, and reflecting on where your organization is and where you need it to be. You need to ensure that you don't overlook the importance of communicating to your employees a high level of respect, both for who they are and for what they contribute to your organization—an action critical to your organization's ability to succeed and thrive.

Indeed, as Barbara L. Fredrickson writes in her book, *Positivity: Groundbreaking Research Reveals How to Embrace the Hidden Strength of Positive Emotions, Overcome Negativity, and Thrive*:

> Flourishing is not a solo endeavor. It's scientifically correct to say that nobody reaches his or her full potential in isolation. Every person who flourishes has

warm and trusting relationships with other people…
and compared with those who languish, people who
flourish spend more time each day with the people
they're close to, and less time alone. Indeed, the tie
between flourishing and enjoying good social relations
is so strong and reliable that scientists have called it a
necessary condition for flourishing.

Recognition—We Know It When We Feel It

Nothing else can quite substitute for a few well-chosen, well-
timed, sincere words of praise. They're absolutely free—and
worth a fortune.

—Sam Walton, founder of Wal-Mart

When it comes to leadership and recognition, one of the first
names that comes to mind is Doug Conant, retired CEO of
Campbell Soup Company and current chairman of both
Avon Products and the Kellogg Executive Leadership Institute
at Northwestern University. Most of us have probably read
at one point or another about how Doug wrote ten to twenty
handwritten notes every day during his time leading Campbell
Soup Company (over 30,000 notes in all) in order to thank his
various employees for their contributions or accomplishments.

For most of us, it's this kind of action that comes to mind
when we think of recognition—that it's a form of positive feedback we can provide to our employees in order to keep them

motivated and engaged while on the job. However, as we'll see in the following series of stories from Doug's tenure at Campbell's, providing recognition as well as a measure of personal accountability is critical to creating a sense of community team wide.

Showing Those You Lead You're Paying Attention

When the global economy started to go into decline, Doug realized that he needed to be more visible in his organization so he reached out to his employees to understand how they were being impacted by the slowdown. Whenever he had a free half-hour in his day he'd put on his sneakers and walk around the company's complex, having conversations with his employees to learn about how they were doing.

Of course, it wasn't just his employees at his company's headquarters that he wanted to reach out to and connect with. Doug also wanted to make sure he was aware of what his employees in other parts of the world were dealing with. To this end, he had an online company portal set up where employees could share their challenges and successes. When his employees began to notice how the successes that were being shared on this portal were being celebrated throughout the company, it was only natural that more of them wanted to get involved and share their experiences as well.

As Doug describes it: "You need to tell people how you're going to behave and then behave that way. And when I was telling people we need to value your individual life journey if we hoped that you would value ours, I implied that I was going to be paying attention to their life journey. And so we developed a practice where we would be surveying all the things that were going right at Campbell—and wrong."[8]

In sending out his ten to twenty notes a day, Doug said that he wanted to accomplish two things. First, he wanted to show his employees that he was personally paying attention to what was going on around them, no matter where in the world they were, because they mattered and what they were doing mattered.

And second, he wanted his effort to show his employees the value of their contributions in terms of the expectations and vision he had for his organization. "Virtually all those notes," he said, "were connected to a specific project where we had high standards, and I'd say, 'Thank you for doing this on time and on budget.'. . . I was reinforcing the standards and I was doing it in a thoughtful way."[9]

As a result, Doug's handwritten notes were soon seen posted on the walls of his employees' cubicles. The notes fostered both a sense of pride in team members' accomplishments and a feeling of belonging because they could see that Doug was paying attention to them and that he cared about their successes.

This also had a trickle-down effect, leading other bosses in the organization to pay more attention to the contributions and efforts of those around them. These leaders became more interested in what those around them were doing and how they could help their colleagues be more successful in their efforts.

In other words, through this seemingly insignificant gesture, Doug was helping to build a culture that fostered a sense of community and belonging, one where employees were no longer looking out for themselves, but as we'll see in the next story, one where they began to look out for each other as well.

Valuing Others to Create Value Within

We are not self-made individuals. We are creations of entanglement, becoming and changing through relationships.

— From *So Far from Home: Lost and Found in Our Brave New World* by Meg Wheatley

In July 2009, Doug was involved in a near-fatal car accident, leaving him with injuries that required four rounds of surgery in the three years following his accident. While Doug was in the hospital, something unexpected happened—he started getting thousands of handwritten notes from his employees all over the world.

In many of them, Doug read how the notes he had sent to his employees over the past few years had made a difference; how this simple gesture from Doug had made them feel like they mattered. They wanted to let him know how much they appreciated him and his leadership and that they wished him a speedy recovery.

While Doug had never expected such a response from his employees, the handwritten notes from his employees had a big impact on himself, his wife, and his family as he worked his way through his recovery: "We have thousands of employee notes that came back to me that brought to light for me the power of reaching out to people in a tough-minded and tender-hearted way, and the power it offers to a leader to create a sense of community that transcends the everyday community that we experience."[10]

What his accident also revealed was how his employees appreciated that the motivation behind his recognition of their efforts was not based purely on the drive to create an engaged workforce. Rather, it arose from a genuine sense of caring and interest in what mattered to them.

As Doug pointed out, "If you don't create that sense of relationship with the people with whom you work and the people with whom you live—in your community and in your family—if you don't create that kind of special connection, it's hard to expect them to have that special connection with the work you're trying to create."[11] Of course, in creating that sense of community, Doug was not only able to create an environment where his employees cared about what happened outside their sphere of influence or control, he also fostered a sense of accountability for their performance in good times and, as we'll see in the next section, in bad times as well.

While meeting with an executive team, Max watched with interest as a senior leader pulled a note out of his wallet to share its contents with the group. It simply read: "I just want you to know I believe in you. —Ms. Mullins, 4th Grade, 1963."

With some emotion, the leader went on to describe why this note was so profoundly important to him, and then he carefully folded it back up and put it back in his wallet.

Using Community to Create Accountability on All Levels

Through perspective, those with humility recognize their connection to the greater whole. They are part of a family, a community, the world, and with that recognition they keep their talents, accomplishments, shortcomings, and failings in perspective.

—From *Leading with Humility* by Rob Nielsen, Jennifer A. Marrone, and Holly S. Ferraro

As a result of his car accident, Doug had to spend the next several months recuperating at the hospital at a time when the economy was leaving his organization with some rather tough challenges. During this time, his team did an admirable job covering for Doug's absence, at times even surpassing the original expectations they had set out for themselves.

And yet, when Doug took a closer look at his team's performance, he found that they were below average as compared to the performance level of their peer group. Although their performance had been exemplary under these current challenges, Doug knew that they could do better than "good enough."

But what bothered Doug the most wasn't just their below-average performance. Instead, it was the fact that the leaders on his team were planning on giving their own teams above-average ratings on their performance because they exceeded those original expectations. They were ignoring the fact that their performance was below-average when compared to their peer groups:

"I was really conflicted. While I was laid up in the hospital, they were working so hard to get our company through this rough patch. And they did! And now I may be returning the favor by saying, 'Thank you very much; your performance was good, but it wasn't good enough.' Ultimately, in my opinion, we should have done better."[12]

Going back to the response his employees gave when they found out about Doug's accident, the fact is that they responded with that level of emotion, concern, and gratitude not because Doug was their CEO. Rather, it was because he had demonstrated in his behavior and actions a high level of interest in each of them and in their ability to succeed. In so doing, he created a sense of community, of something that was bigger than any single one of them, something for which each of them had to take responsibility to maintain, nurture, and develop.

Still, Doug realized that as much as we need to recognize when our employees succeed, we also need to help them recognize when they've missed the mark. And we need to do this in a non-discouraging manner, a manner than encourages them to aim for better the next time.

Exemplifying how leaders need to walk the talk and show consistency in their behavior, after two weeks of deliberation, Doug decided to give both his immediate team members and himself a below-average performance rating. He wanted to show his team that, even though he had a legitimate reason for his below-average performance, his commitment and focus was to his organization's community, and, with it, his accountability to those he lead.

In so doing, he got his team to realize that if he wasn't going to cut himself some slack, they shouldn't either. Their sense of accountability should not simply stop with themselves. On the contrary, their sense of accountability should be tied to their community—to the thousands of employees who looked to them to help in their quest "to create high-performance communities that will make an impact on the world."[13]

"If you're asking people to do extraordinary things, they have to see you leaning in to help them learn and grow. Otherwise, your message will fall on deaf ears over time."[14]

Understanding Your Motivation to Recognize Others

There are many who know what they want to get, but few who know what they want to give.

—Doug Conant, retired CEO, Campbell Soup, Chairman, Avon Products

Doug's story reveals that his act of writing all those handwritten notes was about more than simple employer-employee recognition.

His actions and the actions of his employees when he was laid up in the hospital and unable to be around his team illustrate that his efforts did more than make people feel good about themselves and the work they do. His words and gestures fostered a sense of community and belonging. His employees felt a genuine level of care and concern for Doug's well-being because he was a member of their community.

Similarly, the fact that Doug was able to get his executive team to take ownership for their low performance by not letting his accident serve as an excuse for his failure to meet his targets illustrates how recognition is not simply about acknowledging when employees get things right. It's also about creating an environment where people are willing to take ownership when things go wrong, and to take this ownership not merely out of a sense of personal accountability, but because their results impact the shared community. Each of us has an innate desire to be a part of something bigger than ourselves, something that allows us to accomplish goals or objectives that allow us to grow and feel like we're making a difference:

> [Employees] want to be in a place where they can have
> an extraordinary sense of community, a place that has
> high standards, and a place that cares about them as
> an individual. A place where they can learn and grow.

And I, for the life of me, can't understand why we can't create communities like that.

We did it at Campbell's, I did it at Nabisco before that. The landscape is filled with companies that are doing that. We need to do it better [and] more companies need to embrace the idea. Because this is the way forward in a very dynamic and challenging world.[15]

While visiting with leaders at a large manufacturing facility, Max was approached by one of the operators who simply said, "I just wish our leaders knew how much we all care about the work we do around here. It would be so much more powerful if they spent more time building us up instead of tearing us down."

Could you imagine the productivity gains if we simply treated each other better?

Fostering a Sense of Community Can Help Us Avoid Leadership Vertigo

They want to be in a place where they can have an extraordinary sense of community, a place that has high standards, and a place that cares about them as an individual. A place where they can learn and grow. And I, for the life of me, can't understand why we can't create communities like that.

—Doug Conant, retired CEO, Campbell Soup, Chairman, Avon Products

In sharing Doug's story about handwriting thank you notes for his employees, our goal is not to say you need to do the same, or even something similar. Rather, what matters here with regards to addressing bouts of leadership vertigo is the reason Doug felt compelled to make this extra effort when giving out recognition to his employees.

As much as the act of writing these notes helped to keep Doug grounded in how the contributions of his employees were helping his organization to succeed, taking the time to handwrite these notes also sent the message to those he lead about the motivation behind this recognition.

Namely, that it was a concrete display of the level of appreciation and gratitude Doug had for their efforts and contributions, as well as reinforcing the reality of how important they were to their organization.

Through this simple act, Doug communicated more than simple recognition—he demonstrated how the power of community can bind our collective efforts around a shared purpose and our drive to succeed together. And he was able to do this because he was mindful of not just how he was communicating with those he lead, but what message he was imparting to them, even via something as simple as a handwritten note.

This mindfulness is why Doug was able to connect a sense of shared ownership and accountability through his actions and words—even when he had the opportunity to cut his team and himself some slack because of his medical condition.

Doug was attentive to ensuring that he was consistent in

what he wanted his employees to understand as being critical to their long-term collective success and ability to thrive.

Indeed, while some might think—like Billy—Doug's efforts are one of those nice-to-have measures that a select few leaders can accomplish, both leaders have clearly shown that such efforts also have a positive and significant impact on the financial health of their organizations. In 2010, when most industries were still struggling to dig out from the Great Recession, Campbell Soup Company made $7.7 billion in sales and a twelve percent increase in earnings over the previous year.

Even now, after his retirement from helming this food industry giant, Campbell Soup Company continues to have the highest employee engagement levels in their industry, a testament to the fact that Doug's efforts served to create a community within the organization that could grow, evolve, and thrive even after he moved on.

In his discussion with Tanveer, Doug made it clear that from his vantage point, leaders and their organizations can no longer afford to overlook or lose sight of the connection between creating a sense of community within their organization and their ability to succeed and thrive in the years ahead:

> I believe that leaders of today have to take the initiative, and they have to genuinely and authentically care about their associates in a way that involves them in the process. And in a way that says I feel good about being here, I feel appreciated, I'm going to lean into this a little harder

and in a little more complete way in order to get the job done because I don't want to disappoint this community. That's a powerful idea. And quite frankly, I don't know how it could work any other way.

And I know there are cynics. But the cynics aren't going to solve the world's problems, I guarantee it. The people that are going to solve the world's problems are builders—people who want to make a difference. The leaders of tomorrow are the people who are going to forge new paradigms for people to work in. And that's what we're talking about here—we're talking about building a better world in the workplace and beyond.[16]

That's why we need to ensure that we're using the questions in this chapter to assess whether we are in fact creating those conditions in our organization. That we're not simply claiming that our organization is a community where everyone has a sense of belonging, but that we're ensuring our actions and words are creating a sense of belonging and a sense of purpose to a degree that enables our employees to bring their discretionary effort to their work.

Much in the same way as leaders like Billy Ray Taylor and Doug Conant, if we increase our awareness of what we're really communicating to our team—as opposed to succumbing to leadership vertigo—we can create an atmosphere in which our employees feel a sense of shared ownership and accountability leading to long-term success for ourselves, our employees, and our organization.

Questions to Consider

1. What are some of the ways I can create a stronger sense of community at work?

2. What would the benefits be if we had a stronger sense of community, respect, and recognition in our workplace?

3. What am I communicating to the team? How does this motivate my team members?

4. Do I really care about the individual people and their contributions to the organization?

5. How will my demonstration of appreciation communicate respect? Am I taking enough time to really celebrate, or is my show of appreciation one of those employee-of-the-month-let's-get-this-over-with exercises?

6. Do I feel a genuine sense of pride in the person's success, or am I secretly uninterested?

7. What is my motive for offering this recognition? Is it truly to appreciate an achievement or a clever way to slide in some criticism?

CHAPTER THREE

LEADERSHIP PRINCIPLE #2:

DEVELOP COMPETENCE

Everybody always talks about how you need to manage your time. You need to manage your energy as well.

—Alan Mulally, president and CEO,
Ford Motor Company

In the previous chapter, we discussed how the leadership principle Build Community serves to ensure that we are providing the kind of environment our employees need to succeed and thrive by fostering a sense of belonging through our actions and words.

In this chapter, we want to shift the lens inward to discuss the next leadership principle, Develop Competence, and how it can help us to address those times when we experience leadership vertigo. To do this, we're going to examine the following questions:

- Why does the way I feel matter?
- How do my energy level and emotions impact the people around me?

As we'll see, the key to finding the answers to these questions is by developing a greater awareness of your energy level on any given day as well as your emotional attitude during day-to-day interactions with those you lead. We'll see how both of these can inadvertently shift you off course from your goals.

Emotional Competence

In his book, *Emotional Intelligence: Why It Can Matter More Than IQ*, Daniel Goleman points out that more than eighty percent of the difference between top-performing leaders and average ones is due to "emotional competence."[1] Emotional competence is defined, in part, as the possession of the social skills required to recognize and respond to emotions, both in yourself and others.

These findings mirror the results of Google's "Project Oxygen," which found that technical competencies ranked last among the eight behaviors found in the best managers. Things like "Be a good coach," "Empower your team," and "Express interest in their success" all seemed like common sense, and yet they weren't as obvious as one might expect.

In a *New York Times* interview regarding the research findings, Google's Laszlo Bock, vice president for people operations, said, "In the Google context, we'd always believed that to be a manager, particularly on the engineering side, you need to be as deep or deeper a technical expert than the people who work for you. It turns out that that's absolutely the least important thing. It's important, but pales in comparison. Much more important is just making that connection and being accessible."[2]

Similarly, when asked what traits he looks for when hiring for leadership positions, John Mackey, CEO of Whole Foods, replied:

> I look for people who have a high degree of emotional intelligence—a high capacity for caring. I think for leadership positions, emotional intelligence is more important than cognitive intelligence. People with emotional intelligence usually have a lot of cognitive intelligence, but that's not always true the other way around. Above all, we want leaders who work hard and care deeply about what they do and the people around them.[3]

As the above illustrates, the reality is that your competency as a leader is no longer solely judged by your technical proficiencies and depth of knowledge, but by how capable you are in relating to those around you in order to facilitate their success. On the face of it, this may seem easy, but research findings would suggest otherwise.

Leadership trainers Jack Zenger and Joseph Folkman report on a study they conducted:

> [We] looked at data from 545 relatively senior executives who participated in recent leadership development programs in three different organizations. . . . Through 360 assessments, they were judged on how skilled they were in the 16 attributes we've found through our research to be most essential to leadership effectiveness (fundamental leadership abilities like inspiring others, communicating effectively, driving for success, and the like). . . .
>
> The flaws most commonly tripping up our at-risk leaders were related to failures in establishing interpersonal relationships. Far less frequent were fatal flaws involved in leading change initiatives, driving for results, and—we're happy to report—character. That might explain how they'd managed to get as far as they had. But past a certain point, individual ambition and results aren't enough. As they climb higher in an organization and the ability to motivate others becomes far

more important, poor interpersonal skills, indifference to other people's development, and a belief that they no longer need to improve themselves come to haunt these less effective leaders the most.[4]

What these findings also reveal is that, while we may at times be aware of our own emotions and how it impacts our energy levels, most leaders unfortunately lack an awareness of the moods of their employees and, consequently, how their emotions are impacting how they approach their work. This in turn impacts how leaders treat the people around them because "empathy relies on self-awareness, and if our self-awareness is weak, our empathy will be weak too," says Chade-Meng Tan."[5]

The bottom line is this: The most important job a leader has is not managing processes. Rather, it's to inspire and empower those under their care to succeed in their efforts, something that's difficult to do if you don't know—or care—who they are or how our actions and emotions impact them.

While a good IQ is obviously helpful, when it comes to successful leadership characteristics, our ability to connect with others—our emotional intelligence—is critical to great results. This is why developing our emotional competence is so important.

A Typical Day at Work

Here's an exercise to take a look at your energy and emotions during a typical day at work. Take a sheet of paper and make three columns on it. Write the tasks you deal with in a typical day down the left hand column.

Next, write the emotions you normally feel for each task in the center column (some examples: tired, excited, happy, depressed, angry, bored). Don't overthink this part. Simply write honestly the emotions you feel when you have to deal with each particular task during your day.

Finally, in the last column, using a scale from 1 to 5, with 5 being the highest, rate your perceived energy level when you perform these tasks.

Read over what you've written and answer the following questions:

- What is my dominant emotion throughout the workday?
- What is my average energy level? Is there anything that surprises me?
- How many positive experiences do I have throughout the day? What is my average daily ratio of positive to negative or neutral experiences?
- What are the characteristics of the tasks that I perform with high energy and positive emotions?

Identify where your energy levels are during the most critical points of your day. Are critical tasks being performed when your energy level is at a low point? As we'll examine over the course of this chapter, this is far more common than one might expect and its impact far greater than we may perceive.

UNDERSTANDING THE POWER OF POSITIVE (AND NEGATIVE) STATEMENTS

The single most important factor in predicting organizational performance—which was more than twice as powerful as any other factor—was the ratio of positive statements to negative statements. Positive statements are those that express appreciation, support, helpfulness, approval, or compliments. Negative statements express criticism, disapproval, dissatisfaction, cynicism, or disparagement. The results from the research revealed that in high-performing organizations, the ratio of positive to negative statements in their top management teams was 5.6 to 1. Five times more positive statements were made than negative statements as high-performing teams engaged in work. In medium-performing organizations, the ratio was 1.85 to 1. In low-performing organizations, the ratio was 0.36 to 1. In organizations that performed poorly, in other words, three times as many negative comments were made as positive comments among top management members.

—From *Positive Leadership: Strategies for Extraordinary Performance* by Kim Cameron

Note: Causal directionality could be projected—results were not merely a product of positive talk resulting from high performance.

Happiness is Contagious

When the leader is in a happy mood, the people around him view everything in a more positive light. That, in turn, makes them optimistic about achieving their goals, enhances their creativity and the efficiency of their decision making, and predisposes them to be helpful.

—From *Primal Leadership: Learning to Lead with Emotional Intelligence* by Daniel Goleman, Richard Boyatzis, and Annie McKee

Empirical evidence suggests that working in a positive climate has substantial positive effects on individual and organizational performance.[6]

—Kim Cameron

In the *Harvard Business Review* article "Are You Sure You're Not A Bad Boss?," Jack Zenger and Joseph Folkman report the ten "fatal flaws that contribute to a leader's failure" based on an analysis of 360-degree feedback evaluations of 30,000 managers.

After reviewing these evaluations, the authors found that the number-one fatal flaw leaders were most criticized for by their employees was a "failure to inspire, owing to a lack of energy and enthusiasm," something Zenger and Folkman point out "was the most noticeable of all their failings."[7] Many leaders perform critical tasks when their energy and emotions are low, mostly because they lack an awareness of how their energy and emotions impact business results. Interestingly, the majority of leaders are most energized and engaged when they are interacting with their employees and when they get out from behind their desks to walk about and listen to what those around them have to say and share. Many of the executives and managers we have worked with pointed out that the highlight of their day was when they were around other people or when they were out on the floor spending time with their employees.

It turns out that spending time on the floor where the work is happening is essential not only for the leader's morale, but for the overall performance of the organization. Of course, this goes counter to the prevailing notion that management doesn't want to talk with their employees or doesn't appreciate those they supervise. And yet, what we've found through our work is that the reason managers and executives are not doing this more is because they don't feel they have the time to do it; that most of their time is taken up attending meetings or doing administrative work when they'd rather be out and about engaging with their team members.

This reflects back to what we wrote in the previous chapter about the leadership principle Build Community with regards to the importance of engendering a sense of a shared purpose, not simply between team members, but also between leaders and team members. Leaders need to feel this sense of connection in order to approach their role with the right level of energy and positivity to help guide their team forward.

HOW DO YOU RESPOND IN A STRESSFUL SITUATION?

Will every day be happy and easy? Of course not, but we do have a choice in how we want to respond during those stressful times. This is something that Max was taught at an early age by his own dad:

"It was a Friday night and I was seventeen years old. My father, an active army man, told me to be home by midnight and I knew that meant 12:01 a.m. was too late. So when I came home at 2:00 a.m. and I saw a light on in the living room, I knew there was a problem. Needless to say, I had created a stressful situation for my parents. My dad had been sitting there for two hours thinking about what he might do or say. As I walked into the house, I stopped in the doorway as my father stood up and came over to me. He pulled something out of his pocket and put it in my hand. I looked down and it was a quarter—twenty-five cents—exactly what was needed to make a call at a payphone at that time. He didn't say a word, instead, he simply put that quarter in my hand and then went to bed leaving me standing in the doorway thinking about how I had just disappointed my parents. While this experience didn't make me perfect, I never disrespected my dad like that ever again."

Is it possible that when stressful situations come into your life you can respond in a better way? What if you could get a better outcome by simply deciding to do things differently than you have in the past? What if you could get a better outcome without even saying a word?

Learning to Charge Your Batteries Throughout the Day

There will be days when nothing goes right. Do yourself a favor, and don't make it any harder than it has to be.

—From *Uncommon: Finding Your Path to Significance* by Tony Dungy and Nathan Whitaker

The majority of your time should be spent managing the energy of your team—getting them to focus and refocus on efforts that have a positive impact on their reality rather than on thoughts that offer no return on investment.

—From *Reality-Based Leadership: Ditch the Drama, Restore Sanity to the Workplace, and Turn Excuses into Results* by Cy Wakeman

If leaders feel more energized and positive about their role when they are interacting with their employees, the question we need to ask ourselves is, how can we make changes to our workflow to ensure we are spending more time on the floor with our teams?

After all, once you're in this high-energy, positive-outlook mindset, you'll be able to work at a higher performance level, allowing you to be more creative, more present, and more patient with those around you.

In fact, as Shawn Achor points out in his book, *The Happiness Advantage: The Seven Principles of Positive Psychology that Fuel Success and Performance at Work*, when people are happy they make better decisions, they do a better job of fostering and nurturing relationships with those around them, and they also give more to those around them, making them more contributors than receivers of what's achieved from the group's collective efforts.[8] Of course, life isn't all roses. When we think of people who are happy in their jobs or happy about the work they do, we may assume that this is because they enjoy every part of what they do. This is doubtful. There are less pleasant, if not unpleasant, aspects to everyone's job.

You don't need to remove the least pleasant tasks from your day. Nor need you ignore them. Simply acknowledge that these tasks don't have to dominate you. Author Barbara Fredrickson suggests that "when you come to accept a negative thought as just a thought—that in time will pass—you've disarmed it. With fuller awareness of how negative thoughts and negative emotions feed on each other, you can choose not to go there. You can both accept a negative thought and choose not to magnify it."[9]

Instead, what you need to do is become more aware of the shifts in your energy and emotion levels and use the high points in your day as moments to recharge your battery and reignite your positive emotions in order to approach those less-desirable tasks with a higher sense of energy and emotion.

When we have something to look forward to, we're more optimistic and more willing to see opportunities instead of obstacles. For example, if you go into a meeting with low energy and low expectations, it's not too surprising that the meeting will seem like a waste of time because your attitude and perception serves to fulfill that outcome.

On the other hand, if you schedule your day so you're able to boost your energy and emotion before such a meeting, you'll see it in a different light because you're bringing more energy and positive emotions along.

Let's say that you have a regular conference call that you usually find boring or a waste of time. What if before that meeting you walked around the floor, listening and engaging with your employees instead of, say, checking your emails or doing paperwork while you wait for the meeting to start?

This way, although your energy might normally be low when approaching such a meeting, you've given yourself a boost so you can be more productive and involved, thereby shifting your perception to see this meeting as time well spent.

The impact of being aware of these shifts in your energy and emotions throughout the day won't solely be on how you experience your day. It will also have a tangible impact on how your employees view your ability to successfully lead them.

Create an Engaged and Thriving Workforce

From 1989 to 2000, HCL was all-conquering, but our past became so beautiful we forgot to look at the future. . . . If you want people to thrive, you must give them something to look forward to.

—Vineet Nayar, CEO HCL IT

So far, we've looked at how our energy and emotions impact our leadership competencies in terms of specific tasks we perform over the course of the day.

Now, we'd like you to look at your day as a whole and consider the following questions:

- Is most of my day negative, and if it is, how is that impacting my performance?
- Are there more positive tasks or functions I can schedule throughout the workday, and if not, what does that say about my work and my relationship with it?
- Do I find myself looking forward to what's to come or is my focus more on just trying to get through the day?

While, at times, we all find ourselves working in a survival mode—those moments or days where our emotions are mostly negative and our energy levels low—the problem we have to be mindful of is when we stay in survival mode for so long that we become debilitated. If you have ever worked in a place where survival mode is routine among the team members, or even just walked into such a place to do business, you know what this feels like.

WHEN YOU CRITICIZE SOMEONE, YOU MAKE IT HARDER FOR THAT PERSON TO CHANGE

"If everything worked out perfectly in your life, what would you be doing in ten years?

"Such a question opens us up to fresh possibilities, to reflect on what matters most to us, and even what deep values might guide us through life. This approach gives managers a tool for coaching their teams to get better results.

"Contrast that mind-opening query with a conversation about what's wrong with you, and what you need to do to fix yourself. That line of thinking shuts us down, puts us on the defensive, and narrows our possibilities to rescue operations. Managers should keep this in mind, particularly during performance reviews.

"As I quoted [organizational theorist Richard]

Boyatzis in my book *Focus: The Hidden Driver of Excellence*, 'Talking about your positive goals and dreams activates brain centers that open you up to new possibilities. But if you change the conversation to what you should do to fix yourself, it closes you down.'

"Working with colleagues at Cleveland Clinic, Boyatzis put people through a positive, dreams-first interview or a negative, problems-focused one while their brains were scanned. The positive interview elicited activity in reward circuitry and areas for good memories and upbeat feelings—a brain signature of the open hopefulness we feel when embracing an inspiring vision. In contrast, the negative interview activated brain circuitry for anxiety, the same areas that activate when we feel sad and worried. In the latter state, the anxiety and defensiveness elicited make it more difficult to focus on the possibilities for improvement.

"Of course a manager needs to help people face what's not working. As Boyatzis put it, 'You need the negative focus to survive, but a positive one to thrive. You need both, but in the right ratio.'"

—Daniel Goleman[10]

Keep One Eye on the Future

Although there's no question that it's critical for leaders to have a clear understanding of the present-day challenges their employees and organization face, the problem is that most organizations and their leaders do so at the expense of maintaining a future focus, one that helps us to frame how our efforts today will serve us in the future.

To help clarify this point, let's take a look at the Workflow Energy Model that follows.

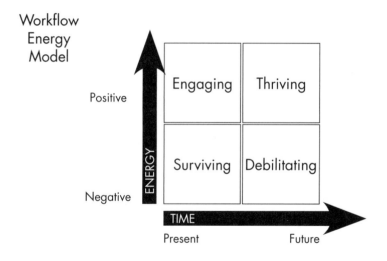

In this diagram we can see that, in the best conditions, the present is about engagement, while the future is about thriving. Certainly, many of us are keenly focused on efforts to ensure our employees are engaged while they are at work. However, what most of us fail to do is to make the connection that our employees are engaged in the present work because of what it promises to bring them in the future.

All of us thrive when we have a bright future to look forward to and we can only do so when we're able to connect what we're doing today with the process of creating or building that desired future. Likewise, our employees become engaged long-term, not because we provide them with a special activity or event, but because of what we're helping them build for tomorrow.

The challenge is that we too often fall into the trap of focusing only on the present, possibly content with the idea that our future will be taken care of, feeling we don't have the time right now to think of the future, or ignoring it all together. This lack of connection to the future makes it difficult to meet today's challenges and is why many organizations find themselves in a slow downward spiral of surviving instead of thriving.

Over time, this leads to a debilitated workforce that simply doesn't care about its organization's goals its objectives.

We need to ask ourselves what we are doing to create something our people can look forward to. Integral to this question is understanding that the present is, to a great degree, dictated by how one feels about the future, because, if we're feeling good about the future, we're going to be more engaged about investing in the present.

This mechanism is exactly what we see in financial investing. When an organization's future is ambiguous, investors are reluctant to invest in its present offerings. But if investors feel good about the organization's future, they invest in the present.

Leaders need to be mindful of the importance of providing employees with a positive—and personally meaningful—vision of the future that will help them with their day-to-day work.

FLOURISHING: THE IMPORTANCE OF POSITIVE EMOTIONS

However much we resist acknowledging it, we humans are not static. We're either on a positive trajectory or a negative one. Either we're growing in goodness, becoming more creative and resilient, or we're solidifying our bad habits, becoming more stagnant and rigid.

People who flourish function at extraordinarily high levels—both psychologically and socially. They're not simply people who feel good. Flourishing goes beyond happiness, or satisfaction with life. True, people who flourish are happy. But that's not the half of it. Beyond feeling good, they're also doing good—and adding value to the world. People who flourish are highly engaged with their families, work, and communities. They're driven by a sense of purpose: they know why they get up in the morning. . . . Although flourishing is noble, it need not imply grand or grandiose actions. It simply requires transcending self-interest enough to share and celebrate goodness in others and in the natural world. Flourishing represents your best possible future. Positivity can help you get there.

—From *Positivity: Groundbreaking Research Reveals How to Embrace the Hidden Strength of Positive Emotions, Overcome Negativity, and Thrive* by Barbara L. Fredrickson

Making It Personal to Help You Succeed

We discovered that emotional intelligence is carried through an organization like electricity through wires. To be more specific, the leader's mood is quite literally contagious.

—From *Primal Leadership: Learning to Lead with Emotional Intelligence* by Daniel Goleman, Richard Boyatzis, and Annie McKee

Emotional competence is something that we've taken for granted—something that we just assume adults have a clear understanding of—and so we don't spend a lot of time building on it. And yet, there's been a number of studies that have shown that just being more present at work—aware of the way we feel and how it impacts those around us—not only impacts how our leadership is perceived by employees, but also makes us happier in that role of serving others. "One of the most central and overlooked principles for lifting others is that our psychological states have an enormous impact on the people around us."[11]

To put it all together, as a leader, you need to communicate and foster a vision of the future which your employees can be positive about so they can be happy and find meaning in their work. In order to accomplish this, you need to discover the peaks and valleys in your energy level and figure out how you can increase your energy to be more present and engaged when interacting with your employees.

The idea is that when we're really happy with where we're at, we are actually more resourceful. When we're more aware of how our energy and emotions impact us and those around us, we're more productive, we're more engaged, we're happier, and we're naturally inclined to look out for those around us as well. This creates a culture of positivity that snowballs.

As professor and leadership expert Dr. Kim Cameron puts it: "Enabling positive emotions . . . fosters a positive climate that, in turn, generates upward spirals toward optimal functioning and enhanced performance. A positive work climate has also been found to enhance decision making, productivity, creativity, social integration, and prosocial behaviors, meaning that individuals and organizations almost always flourish when a positive climate is present."[12]

We often talk about the benefits of positivity in the workplace, but what most of us don't make time for is examining and evaluating what that looks and feels like for our organization. Our goal with this chapter has been to get you to take the time to look at your operation and ascertain for yourself whether it's as positive as could be expected. If you find it lacking, you can be more productive and present for your team by identifying the positive, high-energy points in your day and arranging those moments to help offset the lower points you'll naturally experience throughout the day.

By becoming more aware of this leadership principle, Develop Competence, you should be able to avoid unnecessary bouts of leadership vertigo. Understanding how to connect with people and build relationships that keep yourself and your workforce positive should make it easier for you to open yourself to alternative, and at times novel, approaches that can help you to better serve your team and improve your chances of attaining your shared goals.

Questions to Consider

1. Did the exercise at the beginning of this chapter bring you a new awareness of your energy and emotions? If so, how will you do things differently?

2. How, in the past, have you appeared in your daily interactions with your team? Positive, negative, or so-so?

3. At what points are you letting your low energy or low emotions impede the performance and connection you have with your employees?

4. Are you aware of the emotions of people around you and how you can help them enable themselves to be more positive and more energized about the work they do?

5. Where does your organization currently reside on the Workflow Energy Model? What can you do to increase engagement and a sense of thriving among your employees?

CHAPTER FOUR

LEADERSHIP PRINCIPLE #3:

EARN CREDIBILITY

Leadership is the art of mobilizing others to want to struggle for shared aspirations.

—Jim Kouzes and Barry Posner

Continuing the inward focus we started in our chapter on Developing Competence, we're going to now look at the third leadership principle that's critical to addressing bouts of leadership vertigo: Earn Credibility. Over the course of this chapter, we're going to examine the following questions:

- What is it like to work with me?

- Do people believe in me?

In particular, we're going to look at how answering these two questions can ensure that we are in fact being aware and present to the needs and concerns of those under our care.

> "The lesson for all leaders is this: earning credibility is a retail activity, a factory floor activity, a person-to-person activity. Credibility is gained in small quantities through physical presence. Leaders have to be physically present, they have to be visible, and they have to get close to their constituents to earn their respect and trust. Leaders who are inaccessible cannot possibly expect to be trusted just because they have a title. Credibility is earned via the physical acts of shaking a hand, leaning forward, stopping to listen, and being responsive. By sharing personal experiences, telling their own stories, and joining in dialogue, leaders become people and not just positions."
>
> —Jim Kouzes and Barry Posner

The Three Cornerstones of Credibility

In their book, *Credibility: How Leaders Gain and Lose It, Why People Demand It*, Jim Kouzes and Barry Posner describe credibility as "the foundation of leadership" through which leaders can gain the trust, support, and confidence of those they lead.

Kouzes and Posner point out that credibility is "about what people demand of their leaders as a prerequisite to willingly contributing their hearts and minds to a common cause, and it's about the actions leaders must take in order to intensify their constituents' commitment. People don't commit themselves to work harder and more effectively for just anyone. . . . they vote with their energy, with their dedication, with their loyalty, with their talent, and with their actions."

"It is amazing how many CEO's actually think they have followers," said a CEO recruiter and large company board member during a leadership retreat.

In Kouzes and Posner's findings, credibility hinges on three fundamentals: honesty, competence, and enthusiasm. As they point out, "Earning and sustaining credibility is not a casual exercise. It requires adherence and devotion to a way of doing things that goes beyond mere acknowledgment of its importance."[1] It isn't just about one's ability to rally the crowd with a motivational speech or an invitation to a company barbeque. We have to be willing to honestly reflect and assess our team's assessment of us as leaders. Do our employees find us credible?

So where does one begin? As Google motivator and author of *Search Inside Yourself* Chade-Meng Tan writes, "It all begins with trust," given that an "absence of trust is the root cause of all other dysfunctions." Trustworthiness begins with our ability to be authentic and self-aware.[2]

What Do We Mean by Authenticity?

Let's start by pointing out that authenticity is not about focusing on presenting "the real you" to the world, an approach that many have associated with authenticity in the last few years. This is a problematic view of authenticity as it narrows the focus far too much to our own internal selves, and fails to take into consideration the impact our interactions have on others.

Such a limited definition of authenticity often serves to facilitate or augment the distorted perception brought on by leadership vertigo.

That's why when we talk about authenticity, we're referring to being genuine in your behavior. Specifically, we mean demonstrating a willingness to share and reveal your imperfections and vulnerabilities, thereby allowing yourself to make mistakes. You should also develop a sense of awareness of how to use these mistakes to improve yourself and those you lead.

Chade-Meng Tan puts it this way:

> When team members trust the intentions of each
> other enough . . . they are willing to expose their
> own vulnerabilities because they are confident their
> exposed vulnerabilities will not be used against them.
> Hence, they are willing to admit issues and deficien-
> cies and ask for help. In other words, they are able

to concentrate their energies on achieving the team's common goals, rather than wasting time trying to defend their egos and look good to their teammates.[3]

If we allow ourselves to be authentic, we're able to own up to the mistakes we make because the vulnerability felt in these moments is lessened by the knowledge that we're building trust and respect with our employees.

The Neuroscience of Authenticity

The more we act a certain way—be it happy, depressed, or cranky—the more the behavior becomes ingrained in our brain circuitry, and the more we will continue to feel and act that way.

—From *Primal Leadership: Learning to Lead with Emotional Intelligence* by Daniel Goleman, Richard Boyatzis, and Annie McKee

From a physical perspective, we know that when people are acknowledged, are truly appreciated for a job well done, oxytocin is released in their brains. Oxytocin, along with dopamine and serotonin, make up the group of feel-good hormones in your brain that help you trust others and feel good around them.

The big question is: Do your teammates feel your praise is authentic? Do they feel the oxytocin flowing?

In author Barbara Fredrickson's choice of terms, is your praise heartfelt? Why does this matter? Author Barbara Fredrickson describes it this way:

> Heartfelt. Take a moment to appreciate this word. To truly feel positivity in your heart requires that you slow down. The pace of modern life is often so relentless that it keeps you focused outward, away from your inner core. Over time, this stance numbs your heart. To increase positivity, you'll need to "unnumb" your heart. Let it feel. Let it be open.
>
> Why does this matter? Because positivity that is not felt—that does not register in your heart or in your body—is empty. It does you no good. It can be downright harmful. Positive words not matched with positive feelings wash the body in stress hormones. Insincere positivity is not positivity at all. It's negativity in disguise. To truly benefit from the gestures of positivity—whether a smile, a touch, or an embrace—you need to slow down and drink in what that gesture means. Make it heartfelt.[4]

Think about that for a moment. If a boss is praising his employees, but people don't believe he is sincere, his actions are "negativity in disguise" and likely doing more harm than good.

Worse yet, leaders who purposefully criticize people create an environment where cortisol—a hormone that promotes protective behaviors—is released instead of the feel-good hormones. The release of cortisol erodes trust—it breaks down our positive feelings towards others.

It's natural for us to have some days when we encourage the release of oxytocin and dopamine in the brains of our employees, while on other days our actions or words encourage the release of cortisol. We can see this in our personal relationships, too. We might enjoy being around our spouse or a friend one day, and then on another day, we find them annoying or we get into an argument and any sense of trust or good feelings about the other person diminishes.

The question then becomes where do you spend most of your time? Is it in the cortisol-related stress area where those you lead perceive a dissonance between your actions and words? Or is it in the oxytocin-dopamine area, where you're authentically reaffirming the value and worth your employees have to you and your organization? With the latter, you are building trust and connectedness, and when cortisol-related moments do arrive, your employees are willing to forgive you because you've built a foundation of trust with those under your care.

We All Fall Short

Self-awareness enables us to own our mistakes, which shows vulnerability. But being vulnerable doesn't make us weak. In fact,

CREDIBILITY LOST

One hundred and fifty executives listened with great interest as the global leader of a 12,000-plus employee organization made his presentation during a retreat. While he spoke with conviction and urgency regarding the importance of relationships, he lost credibility when he stated: "I look forward to speaking with each of you individually during the course of the day."

Needless to say, everyone knew he could never deliver on such a statement and it immediately eroded his influence and his credibility.

It takes a good deal of time to build credibility but it can be lost in a few seconds.

it is our personal strength that enables us to admit to having made a mistake. This actually makes us endearing to others because it demonstrates a sense of humility, approachability, friendliness, and connectedness, and that's what being authentic is really all about. It's not about being you for the sake of you, but how you show up and engage with others and take accountability for what those interactions give rise to.

"The credibility-strengthening process hinges upon the belief that human beings should be personally accountable for their own actions. People are held accountable against the standard of shared values upon which there has been agreement.

Ignoring this precept, as many leaders have, by not accepting the consequences of their own actions is exactly what contributes to increasing levels of cynicism, followed by apathy."[5]

Apologize Authentically

When you apologize with real authenticity, you use language that communicates that you are taking ownership of your mistake. This creates a resonance that feels satisfying to both parties. When an apology doesn't feel real because, say, you're subtly casting blame onto others or have your mind on something else, your apology will sound disingenuous and you and the other party will feel a dissonance.

We have seen this many times. A leader will have apologized believing he's done what's necessary to rectify the situation, yet the employee perceives that the boss is saying one thing and feeling another.

Your employees will respect you more and be more willing to forgive you when they see that you're being authentic in accepting accountability for your mistakes.

Integrity

Being authentic also means demonstrating a high level of integrity—being willing to stand for what you believe, for what matters to you. By doing this, you become more consistent in your message because your starting point remains the core values by which you live and define your leadership.

Awareness is a Differentiator

"Don't kid yourself into thinking that your authentic self, unleashed in all its glory, is your key to effective leadership."[6] Real authenticity means that we not only are true to who we are but we have an awareness of how we appear to those around us. Seen in this context, we can understand how authenticity and awareness go hand in hand, as authenticity without awareness is really just arrogance. And this arrogance leads to blind spots that don't serve anyone well.

Dealing With Blind Spots in Our Awareness

You've likely worked with people who don't think they have any blind spots—some even take pride in their own arrogance. The damage done by these folks is hard to measure, but the real costs are higher for the team and the organization than many realize or care to admit. Unfortunately, not all blind spots are obvious. The more subtle the blind spot, the more difficult it can be to uncover. Why? Because our self-awareness is often not as robust as we think it is.

Of course, this doesn't mean we can't take measures to address this gap in our awareness. Stanford management professor

HOW DO YOU RATE?

One challenge we all face in alleviating our leadership vertigo is that we think we're doing better than we really are. In his article "The Success Delusion," Marshall Goldsmith points out that when he asked more than 50,000 of his training program participants to "rate themselves in terms of their performance relative to their professional peers, 80 to 85 percent rank themselves in the top 20 percent of their peer group, and about 70 percent rank themselves in the top 10 percent."[7] Where do you rank yourself?

Robert Sutton points out that "the most effective bosses devote enormous effort to understanding how their moods, quirks, skills, and actions affect their followers' performance and humanity. They regularly ask: What is it like to work for me?"[8]

It's by developing this awareness that we can answer the following questions: Do I actually adhere to the values and beliefs that matter to me? Are they reflected in my behaviors, actions, and what I communicate?

It's easy, for example, for us to say that one of our core values is respect. And yet, when we engage people, we might do so in a disrespectful fashion because we're under a lot of stress or because we have certain results we need to deliver. In those cases, while we might think respect is one of our core values, it's clearly a conditional value to those we serve.

This is why it's important that we increase our awareness of any blind spots regarding how we're engaging with our teams and the impact our blind spot is having on them.

Of course, the danger with blind spots is that they revolve around what we don't know we don't know. And that's why one of the best things we can to do is to ask someone we trust to have an honest conversation about values that he or she feels tend to be in our blind spots. We should also do a bit of soul searching, making sure our core values are what and where we want them to be.

In other words, we have to look both inside and outside in order to understand how we appear to our team. It's through such reflection and inquisitiveness that we discover and learn about our blind spots and what we can do to address them.

While we sometimes have little control over how others perceive a situation, we can become more aware of whether we're meeting our own expectations or not.

The truth is, "hypocrisy is easier to see in other people than in ourselves."[9]

Fostering Creativity and Innovation through Greater Awareness

Leaders exercising humility know that self-awareness brings an element of vulnerability. Once you know your strengths and weaknesses, you are obligated to act on them in some way. If you now see that there is an area that is impeding performance, you must address the deficiency either by gaining the necessary skills, challenging an existing framework, or expressing your need for others to fill in the gap in your own knowledge or skill base. Similarly, now that you are aware of your strengths, you must bring them to bear on the problems at hand. You can no longer stand on the sidelines. Being self-aware challenges us to act based on our strengths and weaknesses.

—From *Leading with Humility* by Rob Nielsen, Jennifer A. Marrone, and Holly S. Ferraro

Acknowledging our mistakes is not permission for us to keep making them, but to demonstrate our awareness of them and our commitment to be better. Even in the process of trying to get better, we're going to make mistakes. Obviously this shouldn't deter us from trying.

Acknowledging our mistakes to our employees and letting them see our efforts to not repeat the same mistakes creates an environment in which our employees are given permission to make mistakes of their own as long as they too learn from them and work to not repeat them.

Fostering such an environment in your organization encourages your employees to be more creative and innovative because they're not afraid of how you or their colleagues will view them if they make a mistake. This attitude creates resiliency—the ability to get back up and continue on. Conversely, when we are afraid of making mistakes in front of our coworkers, we restrain ourselves and our performance, which limits the outcomes we can achieve.

Building and sustaining creativity and innovation has to be intentional, and that requires an organizational culture where authenticity is the norm and awareness leads the way. There has to be a lot of thought, care, deliberation, and attentiveness put into the process so that your employees have permission to explore and make mistakes. Your employees need to see from your own actions that if they're not making mistakes that they can learn from, that means that they're not trying hard enough to improve and grow.

Renewing Credibility—A Continuous Human Struggle

Kouzes and Posner remind us that credibility is "a continuous human struggle"; that we need to commit ourselves to making the effort to build, nurture, and sustain healthy working relationships with those we lead. As leaders, we have to remind ourselves that "the gift of another's trust and confidence is well worth the struggle and [is] essential to meeting the challenges of leading people to places they have never been before."[10]

In summary, when it comes to building and maintaining our credibility as a leader, it's important that we demonstrate our willingness to discover and take responsibility for our part in creating any dissonance our employees may be experiencing between our words and actions and their *perceptions* of our words and actions; that we open ourselves up to critical introspection to gain an understanding of what it's really like to work with us.

Being aware is as much about what you don't know as what you do know. Your employees' perception of your words and actions has as much impact as the words and actions themselves.

In terms of leadership vertigo, the difference between the reality you perceive and the reality your team and organization experiences is the cause of the vertigo.

By keeping the leadership principle Earn Credibility on your radar, you can become more conscious of how leadership vertigo may be preventing you from recognizing the gap between what you perceive and what your employees perceive, a gap that can very quickly erode the credibility you have in the eyes of those under your care.

Questions to Consider

1. What is my motive with those I lead?

2. How do I discover or reveal the blind spots in my leadership?

3. Do I really have all the information or is my mind simply filling in the gaps?

4. How will I hold myself accountable for what I've learned?

5. On a scale of 1 to 5, how do I rate my performance over the past week?

6. Where is the creativity of my team based on my recent words and actions?

CHAPTER FIVE

LEADERSHIP PRINCIPLE #4:

CULTIVATE COMPASSION

A growing body of research suggests that the way to influence—and to lead—is to begin with warmth. Warmth is the conduit of influence: It facilitates trust and the communication and absorption of ideas.

—From *Connect, Then Lead* by Amy J.C. Cuddy, Matthew Kohut, and John Neffinger[1]

As we arrive at the final leadership principle, we'd like to once again shift the focus outward to help you reflect and assess what kind of working environment you're creating for your team to operate in.

In this chapter, we're going to build on the insights we shared from discussing the leadership principles Build Community, Develop Competence, and Earn Credibility to examine how this last leadership principle, Cultivate Compassion, can help us to be more attuned to the needs of our employees and those we serve outside our organization.

In bringing the focus back to the relationships we have with those we lead, we're going to examine the following questions in terms of how they can help us to ensure that we're not confusing the false signals brought on by leadership vertigo with what our employees really require from us to succeed and thrive:

- How am I helping my employees to do their best work?
- How am I able to help them grow?

As we'll see over the course of this chapter, the answers to these questions lie both in how effective we are in consistently listening to what our employees tell us, and in learning from them what it's like to work for us. Only then can we do a better job leading them.

What Does Compassion Look Like at Work?

If you move through the world only with your intellect, then you walk on only one leg. If you move through the world only with your compassion, then you walk on only one leg.

But if you move through the world with both intellect and compassion, then you have wisdom.

—Buddist monk Maha Ghosanadra

Before we look at compassion in terms of its role in today's workplaces, let's first clarify what we mean by compassion and, in particular, how it differs from our understanding of empathy. The *Merriam-Webster Dictionary* defines compassion as a "sympathetic consciousness of others' distress together with a desire to alleviate it." Now, when we talk about being empathetic to others, what we're basically saying is that we know and understand what others are going through—perhaps because we've experienced something similar—but that doesn't necessarily mean that we're compelled to act on it.

Compassion, on the other hand, is not only about demonstrating our understanding and awareness of another person's reality or experience, but also of our willingness to do something about it; to respond or change our approach because of what we now know about the other person's circumstances.

In other words, empathy is understanding that someone just had a bad day; compassion is reaching out to help them do something about it.

Recently, while traveling to an engagement for GE, Max was waiting for a flight in the Atlanta airport. As usual, the waiting area was overcrowded with people waiting to board the plane, including a lady who was traveling with two small kids and lots of luggage. She was obviously overwhelmed with the task at hand, and yet no one seemed interested in helping her—including Max.

Suddenly, a businessman approached this young mother and offered to carry her bags. While reflecting on this gesture of compassion and service, Max realized that the businessman was his client. Here was an executive corporate officer for the General Electric Company offering a hand when no one else was. Needless to say, it was a great reminder to Max of this chapter's principle, Cultivate Compassion.

So what does compassion mean when it comes to work? How does compassion manifest itself in how we lead or guide our organizations when our efforts are not measured by the level of compassion we exhibit or act on towards those under our care?

Here again authenticity comes into play. Our team members can feel our lack of genuine interest in learning about their problems and concerns if we simply parrot a few questions we read in a book on popular psychology. This creates a clear disconnect between what we are saying and how it's supposed to make them feel.

Consider, for example, the common experience we have when we call a customer service line and get a scripted welcome greeting asking us how they can help. Although the words imply that the person on the other side is there to help us, how many of us actually feel like they're really interested in being of help? Do their words come off as genuine and outward-focused, or does it feel more like an automated greeting said without much thought or intent?

On the other hand, when customer service personnel do care, when they truly want to understand what's going on and how they can help, we can feel it. We feel like they're really invested in helping us to achieve our desired outcome. Often this is thanks, in part, to follow-up questions they ask, but much of it is how present they are in that moment, connecting with us.

With forty consecutive years of profitability, Southwest Airlines has differentiated itself from the competition in a number of ways. While they would be the first to admit that they aren't perfect, would it surprise you that one of the ways they differentiate themselves is through compassion? Not just for the customers they serve, but for their employees as well?

Southern California resident Mark Dickinson experienced Southwest's compassion firsthand. Mark had just learned that his injured grandson, Caden, who resided in Colorado, would be taken off life support within hours. While Mark rushed to the Los Angeles Airport so he could be at his grandson's side, his wife called Southwest.

As luck would have it, Mark encountered a long line at the security checkpoint. "I was kind of panicking because I was running late, and I really thought I wasn't going to make the flight," Dickinson told KABC Channel 7 in Los Angeles.

Not only did Southwest hold the plane, but the pilot and gate agent both waited at the gate for Mark to arrive. Upon arrival at the gate, Mark said, "Thank you so much. I can't tell you how much I appreciate this." To which the pilot responded, "They can't go anywhere without me and I wasn't going anywhere without you."[2]

While the circumstances of Mark's urgent travel plans were prompted by a family tragedy, it was the willingness of at least three different Southwest employees to act with compassion that made it possible for him to make his flight. Had any one of these employees decided that this wasn't a request worth their time, we wouldn't know about this story today. In fact, it was only after Mark shared the story himself that it became public knowledge.

Since hearing this story, Max, during the course of his work with Southwest Airlines, had the opportunity to meet with the pilot who held the plane. The pilot prefers to remain anonymous since, as he put it, "that is just the way we do things here. We care about each other and the people we serve."

It is our experience that in interactions with companies that continue to be praised for great customer service by both the public and industry experts, there's little scripted or pre-packaged in the conversations they hold with their clientele. Instead, they're driven by a level of compassion to understand what is needed of them and then, acting upon this knowledge, to find some way to create the outcome those they are helping hope to attain.

While we might think that being compassionate to others benefits those others more than it does us, the reality is, we, as leaders, also gain a host of benefits from employing compassion. Pragmatically, any emotional trials employees might be experiencing in their personal lives can impact how they approach their work and the level of discretionary effort they're able to commit to our organization's goals.

Showing compassion at work encourages a healthier workplace because we are demonstrating to our employees that we care about them as people. Benefits to our organization include:

• Greater focus on shared goals
• Better overall results
• Improved camaraderie
• Increased levels of trust and respect

Indeed, research has shown that experiencing compassion at work leads to a cascading effect of positive emotions among employees, leading to reduced stress levels, a decline in employee turnover rates, and an increase in job satisfaction—all of which give rise to a tangible improvement to an organization's bottom line and overall productivity.[3] Again, looking at some of today's thriving organizations, we can clearly see that one of the main driving forces behind their continued success stems from the commitment shown by their leaders to encourage compassion in their organization.

Of course, driving compassion in your workplace requires more than memorizing some quick, easy-to-do steps. As we'll see over the course of this chapter, what this leadership principle really requires is a greater sense of mindfulness in listening to what our employees have to say and a greater willingness to demonstrate that we want to learn more about the whole persons they are.

Listening—Where Compassion Begins

Prioritizing warmth helps you connect immediately with those around you, demonstrating that you hear them, understand them, and can be trusted by them.

—From *Connect, Then Lead* by Amy J.C. Cuddy, Matthew Kohut, and John Neffinger[4]

If we cultivate compassion in our leadership—if we're authentic in how we show compassion to address the various opportunities and problems our employees bring to our attention—then listening becomes a genuine action. It's no longer something we do as a prescriptive or stop-gap measure to address issues that crop up. Rather, it becomes a reflection of the inner principles and beliefs that we use to guide our actions and behaviors.

In many ways, the act of becoming a better listener is where compassion begins because it compels us to be outward-focused. Our efforts shouldn't be limited to how we lean forward when listening to someone or how often we repeat back what they tell us. Rather, our focus should be on trying to understand the realities of what the other person is facing and what we can do to help them address them.

A title may put you in front of the room, but it isn't why people listen.

—S. Max Brown

We shouldn't enter conversations where compassion is warranted armed with our own assumptions of what needs to be done. This can waste limited time, attention, and resources on a solution that might not be what an employee requires. Instead, we should go into these conversations with a sense of curiosity and a desire to understand their perceptions and realities, and to help them to discover the best solution. In this way, we're able to engender both a sense of respect and trust.

Of course, there will be times when our employees will see things differently than we do. But showing compassion and taking the time to understand their position will demonstrate our willingness to consider their opposing views.

There is a truism that employees are not driven to be right; rather, they are driven to be heard. It's for this reason your employees often argue or jostle for political points—not necessarily because they disagree with what you want to accomplish or your methods, but because they don't feel heard regarding the issues at hand. They feel disconnected from the process of making your vision a reality, which naturally leads to a decreased sense of value for the contributions they make towards your shared purpose.

Instead of Listening More, Listen More Effectively

Humility keeps our egos from getting in the way of our senses. A humble person can see and hear and feel more clearly.

—From *So I'm Not Perfect: A Psychology of Humility*
by Robert J. Furey

It's important that we note that this ability to be more compassionate by listening to those around us doesn't have to be an intensive, time-dependent action. It's not about adding more to your leadership plate. Rather, it's about being more attentive in those day-to-day moments to ensure that we are genuinely listening to what our employees are telling us instead of formulating our response or thinking ahead to what we have to do next.

This mirrors what we discussed in the chapter on the leadership principle Develop Competence: Our energy and emotional levels can impact our competency in performing the critical tasks we face at a given time on a given day. It's not just about the amount of time we spend. If we approach employee interactions in a negative mood, or with low energy, it becomes very hard for us to demonstrate and feel compassion.

On other hand, if we ensure that, when we have these conversations, our energy levels are high and we have a positive outlook, it's much easier to be attentive in trying to understand the realities our employees face and to help them overcome any hurdles to success.

Learning is the Key to Compassion

Our capacity to grow determines our capacity to lead.

—From *Great Leaders Grow*
by Ken Blanchard and Mark Miller

The key to sustained success is to keep growing as a team. Winning is about moving into the unknown and creating something new.

—From *Eleven Rings: The Soul of Success* by Phil Jackson and Hugh Delehanty

In discussing the role listening plays in our ability to demonstrate compassion, there's an obvious underlying thread connecting all of this. That is, our ability to effectively listen to what others are telling us is dependent on how curious we are to learn from them and from what we see going on around us.

Researchers have found that our motivation to learn or discover new information is often dependent on our awareness of "information gaps" in our knowledge or understandings, which we then actively seek to fill. Conversely, if we think we have all the facts about a topic, we lack the motivation to seek new information or ideas regarding it.[5]

This phenomenon is evident when we get comfortable with our past successes and rely on the same patterns of behavior as we move forward. Professors Ryan and Robert Quinn warn us: "Organizational members are right when they assume that their competencies made their success possible. But when they focus on applying their competencies over and over again instead of on continually learning and improving, those competencies can take on a life of their own. Members ignore feedback in favor of revering these cherished competencies. If they ignore feedback long enough, they plunge their organizations into failure."[6]

Ignoring feedback and relying on competencies without mindfulness may be a sign one is suffering from a bout of leadership vertigo. Learning, as an element in the leadership principle Cultivate Compassion, can help alleviate this because it reminds us that growing is about learning—it's about coming to a new understanding or the revealing of something you didn't know or weren't aware of.

By employing this leadership principle, you can ensure that your focus when listening to your employees is on discovering what obstacles they face that are impeding their ability to complete the tasks you assigned them. Here it helps to ask yourself this question: How am I responsible for their inability to accomplish the task? While you might not have initially been aware of these challenges, now that you've learned about them, you can help your employees to overcome them by providing additional resources or insights.

Of course, we have to be honest in admitting that there will be times where we don't have the answers to help our employees overcome the challenges they face. Although it can be difficult at times to admit this to our employees, employing compassion in your leadership can help you to overcome this problem, which is what we'll examine in the next section of this chapter.

A Leader's Dilemma—Addressing the Need to Have All the Answers

> To realize that you do not understand is a virtue; not to realize that you do not understand is a defect.
>
> —Lao Tzu

One of the biggest challenges leaders face is admitting to your employees that you don't have all the answers. Part of the reason for this issue is that most organizations continue to treat leadership as a reward for employees who demonstrate technical proficiencies that the organization requires to remain innovative and competitive. Of course, the reality is that no one—regardless of his or her position or title—can have all the facts or information about every facet of an organization and consequently no one person can have all the answers. The best leaders learn to delegate authority and decision-making to others in order to ensure that the correct, informed decisions are being made.

Still, it can be daunting to admit to your employees that you don't have the answers to the problems they're currently facing. But this is where the leadership principle Cultivate Compassion comes in because it encourages us to lead with curiosity; we don't need to view not having all the answers as a sign of weakness, but as an opportunity to learn from our employees.

Going back to what the researchers have shown regarding learning and curiosity, by being more willing to admit we have gaps in our awareness and understanding, we're able to be more attentive in listening to what our employees have to say because we're curious to learn what's missing in those information gaps.[7]

Encouraging this sense of curiosity in our leadership allows us to be far more supportive and influential than if we tried to look like we have already learned everything we need to know. Besides, if we are willing to admit we have gaps in our awareness and understanding, we are less likely to be tempted to bluff our way through a situation.

We don't mean to suggest that it's about ignoring or overlooking what your own experiences and insights inform you about a situation. Instead, it's about making sure you're not relying exclusively on your own answers—or worse, assumptions—to inform your decisions.

It's about developing an awareness of the information gaps and blind spots we all have and learning not to react to them in a judgemental fashion. Being able to develop this awareness and acting on it will go a long way in helping you to overcome those false signals that leadership vertigo creates in your brain.

Learning from Mistakes

Your value lies not in status or title, but in the roots of your character and depth of your compassion.

—From *Walking with Justice* by Dr. Mollie Marti

Another benefit that arises from bringing more compassion to your leadership—in being more open to learning from your employees' insights and experiences—can be seen in the impact it will have on how you respond in those instances when things inevitably go wrong. When mistakes are made or your organization experiences a failure, you'll be less likely to focus on assigning blame or fault to minimize any damage to your leadership.

Without compassion, it becomes easier for us to cast blame, to criticize, and even to marginalize the contributions and efforts of those around us because we're looking at the situation solely from our vantage point and not taking into account the perspectives of those around us.

When we lead without compassion, we pay more attention to preserving our status as leader—ensuring our employees see us as having all the answers, even when we know we don't—because our focus is on retaining control and power so that others will have no choice but to follow us.

Instead, by using compassion, your train of thought will be on those information gaps in your awareness and understanding. Your response will be focused more on listening to what your employees have to say about what happened and learning from those insights so you can help your employees ensure this doesn't happen again.

This principle ties back to what we saw in our discussion of the leadership principle Build Community—of the importance of fostering a sense of community and belonging among your employees because you share with them a sense of shared purpose *and* accountability.

By using the leadership principle Cultivate Compassion to help guide our actions and inform what we do, our focus shifts outward, allowing us to tap into our innate curiosity so we can hear, understand, and act on what our employees tell us. When your employees see that you're operating from this mindset, they will become less concerned about avoiding blame. Instead their focus will be directed towards measures or insights they can provide to help resolve the situation and help your organization to move forward.

Compassion—It's More than Simply the Right Thing to Do

Seeing goodness strengthens the affective and cognitive components of compassion. When you instinctively and habitually perceive goodness in everyone, you instinctively want to understand and feel for them.

—From *Search Inside Yourself: The Unexpected Path to Achieving Success, Happiness (and World Peace)* by Chade-Meng Tan

As humans, it's a natural response for us to become protective of our status when we feel threatened or are faced with uncertainty. However, as today's most successful leaders know and understand, the key to moving beyond simply surviving to thriving in today's complex, global economy is not by leading our organizations based solely on what we know. Rather, it's by having the willingness to open ourselves up to truly listen, understand, learn, and act on the insights and experiences of others, especially those under our care.

We all understand that compassion is important; that it's good to have in our lives and it's the right thing to do. But beyond compassion being something nice to have in your organization, research has demonstrated that employing compassion through your leadership provides a tangible, empirical difference in how your employees approach their work and in how it can give your organization a leading edge and differentiator. This will show up both in how you do business and in your bottom line.

Indeed, employing the leadership principle Cultivate Compassion will help you to address some of the false signals leadership vertigo creates about what's really going on in your organization. Actively listening to your employees and learning from what they have to share will allow you to have a better understanding of the realities your employees face and, consequently, where you need to put your time, energy, and focus.

Questions to Consider

1. When things go wrong, what is my initial response? To cast blame and fault or to listen and learn from my employees about their insights and experiences that lead to this failure?

2. What do I do that prevents my employees from doing their best work?

3. Do I engender a learning environment where employees feel they'll be listened to?

4. What information am I missing in the decisions I make, and do I feel threatened by these information gaps? Why is that?

5. What am I choosing to become defensive about? Why am I becoming defensive about it?

6. Are there moments where the information I get from my employees doesn't match up with my perceptions of the situation? What's behind this?

CHAPTER SIX

WHERE DO WE GO FROM

HERE?

The day began just like any other day—people got up and ate breakfast, preparing themselves for another day at work. Children packed their lunches and their homework and headed off to school, while shopkeepers opened their stores in anticipation of the daily throng of commuters who'd make their way under the dull, grey sky that hung above.

While the day may have started out like any other, for the inhabitants of the Sichuan province in southwest China, May 12, 2008, would turn out to be one of the saddest days in their nation's history. Later that afternoon, shortly after lunch, this province of China was hit by an 8.0 magnitude earthquake—an earthquake that was so strong, its tremors were felt as far away as India. An earthquake that killed nearly 70,000 people and left more than five million people homeless.

Nine-year-old Lin Hao was walking down the corridor of his school, Yuzixi Primary School, with two of his classmates when the first major tremor hit. As the ground shook below his feet, the building that had been his second home came crashing down on him and his other classmates, burying the children in a mountain of concrete debris and steel.

Fortunately, Lin Hao was able to dig himself out of the rubble and soon found himself standing on top of the remains of his school, taking in the almost-alien landscape of what was once his home town Yingxiu, seeing the places he used to play with his friends, and the neighborhood where his parents and his home used to be.

It wasn't just the physical landscape that had changed, though. Gone along with the buildings were the sounds of the bustling crowds and the ringing of bicycle bells as people made their way through the town's streets. Now there was nothing but an eerie silence punctuated by the sounds of falling debris, and the moans and cries of anguish from those who now found themselves trapped under the ruins of their workplaces and homes.

Taking in the destruction and loss that lay before him, it wouldn't have been surprising if Lin Hao ran from the ruins of his school in desperate search of his parents and other family members. In the face of such horror, who wouldn't want to seek out the safety and comfort of those we love?

And yet for Lin Hao, now was not the time to seek comfort and security. He turned back to the pile of rubble and debris that he had dug himself out of and begun pulling away at the concrete rocks and metal rods to help free his other classmates.

As he pulled and tugged at the concrete ruins around him, Lin Hao was struck by a piece of debris from above which sliced a deep gash on the right side of his head. Undeterred, Lin Hao continued to try and pull the debris apart, slashing both his arms on the sharp and jagged edges of the concrete rubble.

Eventually, Lin Hao found the two classmates who were walking with him down the school corridor when the earthquake hit and he helped them out from under the debris and off to safety. Having pulled his two classmates from the rubble, Lin Hao began to search the rest of the ruins of the school building, calling out to his classmates and teachers in the hopes of finding other survivors buried under the rubble.

His efforts soon paid off as he located a group of his classmates crying out for help, their sobs muffled by the weight of the concrete that they were buried under. Try as he might, Lin Hao couldn't get his classmates out—the concrete debris was simply too big for him to move. So Lin Hao did the only thing he could do . . . he sat down as close as he could to one of the gaps where his trapped schoolmates could hear him and he encouraged them to sing songs with him while they waited for help to arrive.

Eventually, help did arrive to dig his trapped schoolmates out and to send Lin Hao to get medical attention before his injuries worsened. Of the thirty-two students who attended Yuzixi

Primary School with Lin Hao, only ten—including the two children Lin Hao helped to free—survived this disaster.

Later, when Lin Hao was asked why he stayed with his trapped schoolmates on top of the school ruins—which at any minute could have crumbled further due to the aftershocks of the earthquake—Lin Hao simply replied: "I was the hall monitor, it was my job to look after my classmates."

More than Doing Better, We Can *Be* Better

Efficiency is doing things right; effectiveness is doing the right things.

—Peter Drucker

In the light of any disaster, it's common to focus on stories where we get to see our collective humanity at its finest; in many ways, it's a natural response to trying to grapple with the magnitude of the loss of human life, and the impact the disaster has had on those left behind in its wake. What makes Lin Hao's story all the more compelling is not just his age, but what his example teaches us about how we view ourselves, and in particular the role we play in guiding those under our care.

Lin Hao's story is not merely a reflection of human bravery and sacrifice; it's also a reflection of what leadership looks like when we do the right things, when we're mindful of ensuring that we don't let the circumstances around us—no matter how grave or daunting—deter us from staying true to what we want our leadership to represent.

Indeed, in Lin Hao's story, we see the four leadership principles we've discussed over the course of this book in action.

In terms of the leadership principle Build Community, we can see that Lin Hao was compelled not to look at the situation in terms of his own self-preservation, but in terms of how he could help those in need because he respected and valued his classmates to the point that he cared deeply about their well-being.

Similarly, through the leadership principle Develop Competence, we can appreciate how he managed his energy and emotional levels by choosing to sit as close as he could to his trapped classmates so he could keep their spirits high by encouraging them to sing with him.

Lin Hao also demonstrated elements of the Earn Credibility leadership principle in that he was mindful of how his actions would impact his classmates because he had a sense of awareness that such a gesture would help them to not lose hope.

And this leads us to the last leadership principle we discussed, Cultivate Compassion. Lin Hao clearly not only empathized with the fears and pain of his trapped classmates, but took measures to show them that they were not alone and that he would not give up on them until help arrived to save them.

The point in sharing Lin Hao's story is not that we should worry about how we would lead our organization if something happened that shook its very foundation. Rather, it's that by inculcating the four leadership principles into our day-to-day words and actions we are creating a culture that will drive our organization to succeed in the best and the worst of times.

It is important that we don't wait for things to go wrong, but that we develop a finely-tuned sense of self-awareness that helps us recognize when we're suffering from a bout of leadership vertigo—times when we are allowing false signals from our brain to deter us from providing what our employees need to succeed and thrive. In so doing, we not only do a better job leading our organization, but we develop a better version of ourselves.

Looking Ahead at How You Will Lead Your Organization

No matter how far you have gone on a wrong road, turn back.

—Turkish proverb

I can't pretend to be an expert in leadership theory. But what I do know is that the art of transforming a group of young, ambitious individuals into an integrated championship team is not a mechanistic process. It's a mysterious juggling act that requires not only a thorough knowledge of the time-honored laws of the game but also an open heart, a clear mind, and a deep curiosity about the ways of the human spirit.

—From *Eleven Rings: The Soul of Success*
by Phil Jackson and Hugh Delehanty

Despite the increasing demands on your time, attention, and resources, it's still possible to become more aware of how you engage and empower your employees and to recognize that bouts of leadership vertigo should not be seen as an excuse for leading your employees in a way that disengages them from committing their discretionary efforts to your shared purpose.

When we become more aware of the leadership principles that can help us manage leadership vertigo, we become more productive, more satisfied, more powerful, and more effective. Many of us have seen or experienced leaders struggling with leadership vertigo, where they grapple with the following questions:

- How come I'm not more effective?
- Why won't my employees forgive me even though I apologized?
- How come they don't believe me?
- How come I'm not coming across clearly?
- Why don't they follow me, or at least do so unwillingly?
- Why do employee surveys report my team is not satisfied with my performance after everything I've done for them?

The Answers Lie in the Questions We Ask Ourselves

As with all the conversations, there may be no immediate and clear answers to these questions. It doesn't matter. The questions themselves work on us, and when they are asked, this work is activated. In the asking, we are creating space for gifts which are central to restoration, restoration that wants to occur at this moment. The questions, in this way, are the transformation, simply by being named.

The power is in the asking, not in the answers.

—From *Community: The Structure of Belonging*
by Peter Block

Over the course of our journey, we've addressed the following questions in our examination of the various leadership principles and how they can help manage the inevitable bouts of leadership vertigo we all experience:

- Do the people who work for me feel like they belong? (Build Community)
- How is my energy impacting them? (Develop Competence)
- Am I authentic in my interactions with my team members and aware of what it's like to work for me? (Earn Credibility)
- Do I truly care about my employees, and do I reach out to help them with their challenges? (Cultivate Compassion)

It's important to remember that the leadership principles we've discussed in this book are not independent. Rather, they are *interdependent* as they work in unison to influence and impact our ability to decipher and identify the false signals which can lead us off course from what we want to accomplish.

By using these leadership principles in concert, you can make sure that:

- Your efforts allow your employees to feel respected and valued as members of a community bound by a shared purpose. (Build Community)
- You know how you show up to engage with your team members in your daily interactions with them. (Develop Competence)
- You're aware of how your actions and words impact those you lead. (Earn Credibility)
- You're actually listening to what others are saying so you can learn from them. (Cultivate Compassion)

When we sat down to write this book, the one thing we both agreed on is that we didn't want to give you a shopping list of steps to graft onto how you approach leadership. Instead, what we wanted to create was a chance for you to reflect on and review your leadership skills, to get you to contemplate and understand any differences that exist between your perception of how you lead your team and the perceptions of those you lead. We want to increase your awareness of how subtle actions can have a tangible impact on those under your care.

Unfortunately, many leaders rely on quick-fix, short-term strategies to help alleviate some of the issues they face in their workplaces. But as study after study has shown—not to mention what we're sure you've seen first-hand in your own organization—such limited methods only serve to perpetuate and magnify the issues.

These half measures are why so many employees sit on the sidelines, unwilling to commit their discretionary efforts whole-heartedly. They've come to discount these management strategies as merely another pet project or lightening-in-a-bottle idea that those in charge expect will somehow turn things around.

Our desire that you contemplate your leadership on additional levels drove our decision to employ a series of questions to examine each of these leadership principles because, as the quote from Peter Block points out, by asking questions we hope to transform you not into the kind of leader we think you should be, but the kind of leader your employees need you to be.

As you use these four leadership principles, your ability to lead will become stronger and more sustainable. You'll recognize the following:

- When you know your employees feel like they belong; that what your actions and words communicate fosters a sense of purpose and meaning in your team's collective efforts.

- When you're aware of the emotional and energy levels you bring to critical tasks throughout your day, and how this impacts how you are perceived in your daily interactions with those you lead.

- When you understand the impact of how your employees perceive your authenticity and accountability has on your organization's success.
- When you demonstrate a sense of compassion that lets your employees know you care about what they experience in their day-to-day lives; that you want them to succeed in their collective efforts; and that you have their back when things go wrong.

The fact is, you will make mistakes. That's not to say that this gives you permission to fail to deliver what your employees need or to not care or accept accountability about those moments when you slip up. Rather, going back to the examples of leaders like Billy Ray Taylor, Doug Conant, young Lin Hao, and the great people at GE and Southwest Airlines, it's about demonstrating your commitment to honoring what you want your leadership to represent.

As we saw over the course of this book, you can become the leader you want to be by increasing your awareness of what's going on in your own mind and how your employees perceive your words and actions. This awareness will work to ensure you're creating the right conditions to help your employees succeed and thrive over the long-term. If they succeed and thrive, so will you and your organization.

Use the four leadership principles daily in order to help you avoid recurring bouts of leadership vertigo. If you do so, we're confident you will find success and happiness in your journey towards leadership excellence.

APPENDIX

Additional Resources

"Leadership Biz Cafe #10—Doug Conant on Leadership and Organizational Success" TanveerNaseer.com, December 4th, 2012.

The Real Recognition Radio leadership library is a rich collection of interviews with global executives, authors, and thought leaders that can be found at Rideau.com and as podcasts in iTunes. Here is a small sample of some of the shows that we drew upon in this book:

Real Recognition Radio interview with Vineet Nayar, "Employees First, Customers Second," hosted by: Roy Saunderson & S. Max Brown, September 24, 2010.

Real Recognition Radio with Doug Conant and Mette Norgaard, "TouchPoints," hosted by: Roy Saunderson & S. Max Brown; May 31, 2011.

Real Recognition Radio with Barbara L. Fredrickson, Ph.D., "Love 2.0," hosted by: Roy Saunderson & S. Max Brown; May 31, 2011.

Real Recognition Radio with Billy Taylor, "Engaging for Real Results," hosted by: Roy Saunderson & S. Max Brown, August 19, 2011.

Real Recognition Radio with Kevin Allen, "The Hidden Agenda," hosted by: Roy Saunderson & S. Max Brown, April 17, 2012.

Real Recognition Radio with Jamie Naughton, "Leadership: Zappos Speaker of the House," hosted by: Roy Saunderson & S. Max Brown, December 4, 2012.

Real Recognition Radio with Jim Kouzes, "Credibility," hosted by: Roy Saunderson & S. Max Brown, March 30, 2012.

Real Recognition Radio with Chade-Meng Tan, "Search Inside Yourself," hosted by: Roy Saunderson & S. Max Brown, June 12, 2012.

Real Recognition Radio with Brene Brown, "Daring Greatly," hosted by: Roy Saunderson & S. Max Brown, May 1, 2012.

Real Recognition Radio with David & Wendy Ulrich, "The Why of Work," hosted by: Roy Saunderson & S. Max Brown, July 27, 2011.

Real Recognition Radio with Anne Kreamer, "It's Always Personal," hosted by: Roy Saunderson & S. Max Brown, April 23, 2013.

Real Recognition Radio with Daniel Pink, "Drive," hosted by: Roy Saunderson & S. Max Brown, November 1, 2011.

Real Recognition Radio with Greg Link, "Smart Trust," hosted by: Roy Saunderson & S. Max Brown, July 10, 2012.

Real Recognition Radio with Shawn Achor, "Happiness Advantage," hosted by: Roy Saunderson & S. Max Brown, April 26, 2011.

Real Recognition Radio with Nick Sarillo, "Great Corporate Culture: A Slice at a Time," hosted by: Roy Saunderson & S. Max Brown, May 27, 2012.

Books We Recommend

Achor, Shawn; *The Happiness Advantage.*

Allen, Kevin; *The Hidden Agenda.*

Amabile, Teresa and Kramer, Steven; *The Progress Principle.*

Andersen, Erika; *Leading So People Will Follow.*

Biswas-Diener, Robert; *The Courage Quotient.*

Blanchard, Ken and Stoner, Jesse Lyn; *Full Steam Ahead*

Block, Peter; *Community: The Structure of Belonging.*

Brown, Brene; *Daring Greatly.*

Brown, Rebel; *Defy Gravity.*

Bryant, John Hope; *Love Leadership.*

Burg, Bob; *Go-Givers Sell More.*

Cameron, Kim; *Positive Leadership.*

Canaday, Sarah; *You According to Them.*

Charmine, Shirzad; *Positive Intelligence.*

Chism, Marlene; *Stop Workplace Drama.*

Conant, Doug and Norgaard, Mette; *TouchPoints.*

Conley, Chip; *Emotional Equations.*

Covey, Stephen M.R. and Link, Greg; *Smart Trust.*

Crowley, Mike; *Lead From the Heart.*

Diaz, Monica; *OtherEsteem.*

Emmons, Robert; *Thanks: The Science of Gratitude.*

Fredrickson, Barbara L.; *Love 2.0.*

Garfinkle, Joel; *Getting Ahead.*

Geisler, Jill; *Work Happy.*

George, Bill; *True North.*

Glanz, Barbara; *Care Packages.*

Grant, Adam; *Give and Take.*

Heffernan, Margaret; *Willful Blindness.*

Hsieh, Tony; *Delivering Happiness.*

Johnson, Whitney; *Dare. Dream. Do.*

Kates, Andrea; *Find Your Next.*

Kawasaki, Guy; *Enchantment.*

Kouzes, Jim and Posner, Barry, *Encouraging the Heart.*

Kreamer, Anne; *It's Always Personal.*

Lapin, David; *Lead By Greatness.*

Li, Charlene; *Open Leadership.*

Lipp, Doug; *Disney U.*

Marcum, David and Smith, Steven; *Egonomics.*

Marciano, Paul; *Carrots and Sticks Don't Work.*

Nayar, Vineet; *Employees First, Customers Second.*

Pink, Daniel; *Drive.*

Quinn, Robert and Ryan; *Lift.*

Rath, Tom and Hartman, Jim; *Wellbeing.*

Sarillo, Nick; *A Slice of the Pie.*

Saunderson, Roy; *Giving: The Real Recognition Way.*

Schwartz, Tony; *The Way We're Working Isn't Working.*

Sharma, Robin; *The Leader Who Had No Title.*

Simmons, Annette; *The Story Factor.*

Spiegleman, Paul; *Patients Come Second.*

Stallard, Michael; *Fired Up or Burned Out.*

Tan, Chade-Meng; *Search Inside Yourself: The Unexpected Path to Achieving Success, Happiness (and World Peace).*

Ulrich, David and Wendy; *The Why of Work.*

Wheatley, Margaret; *Turning Toward One Another.*

Wiseman, Liz; *Multipliers.*

NOTES

Chapter One—Understanding Leadership Vertigo

1. "The State of the American Workplace: Employee Engagement Insights for U.S. Business Leaders." Gallup Report, 2013.

2. "2012 Global Workforce Study: Engagement at Risk: Driving Strong Performance in a Volatile Global Environment." Towers Watson. http://www.towerswatson.com/en-CA/Insights/IC-Types/Survey-Research-Results/2012/07/2012-Towers-Watson-Global-Workforce-Study.

3. "NTSB Accident Report NYC99MA178." 1999. http://www.ntsb.gov/aviationquery/brief.aspx?ev_id=20001212X19354.

4. "Lost? Go Vest, Young Man." *Wired*. June 8, 2001. http://www.wired.com/gadgets/miscellaneous/news/2001/06/44376.

5. Phelps, Mark. "Vertigo Can Be Deadly." *Flying*. July 15, 2009. http://www.flyingmag.com/pilot-technique/tip-week/vertigo-can-be-deadly.

6. Ericsson, K. Anders, Michael J. Prietula, and Edward T. Cokely. "The Making of an Expert." *Harvard Business Review*. July–August 2007.

Chapter Two—Leadership Principle #1: Build Community

1. "Engaging for Real Results." Real Recognition Radio with Billy Taylor. Hosted by Roy Saunderson & S. Max Brown. August 19, 2011.

2. Ibid.

3. Ibid.

4. Ibid.

5. Ibid.

6. Ibid.

7. "Why You Should Sit with More People in the Lunchroom." *Harvard Business Review*. The Daily Stat. July 27, 2012. http://web.hbr.org/email/archive/dailystat.php?date=072712.

8. "Doug Conant: Leadership is a sacred task." Nature of Business Radio. July 22, 2012. http://www.greenbiz.com/blog/2012/07/22/doug-conant-leadership-sacred-task.

9. "Doug Conant on Leadership and Organizational Success." Leadership Biz Cafe #10. December 4, 2012. http://TanveerNaseer.com.

10. Ibid.

11. Ibid.

12. Conant, Douglas and Mette Norgaard. *TouchPoints: Creating Powerful Leadership Connections in the Smallest of Moments* (2011), 76.

13. "The Thought Leader Interview: Douglas Conant." *Strategy+Business*. Issue 68. Autumn 2012.

14. Ibid.

15. "Doug Conant on Leadership and Organizational Success." Leadership Biz Cafe #10. December 4, 2012. http://TanveerNaseer.com.

16. Ibid.

Chapter Three—Leadership Principle #2: Develop Competence

1. Goleman, Daniel. *Working with Emotional Intelligence*. (New York: Bantam, 1998).

2. Bryant, Adam. "Google's Quest to Build a Better Boss." *The New York Times*. March 12, 2011.

3. Inc Staff. "John Mackay of Whole Foods on Hiring Leaders." June 30, 2009. http://m.inc.com/?incid=34.

4. Zenger, Jack and Joseph Folkman. "Good News: Poor Leaders Can Change." *Harvard Business Review*. January 2013. http://blogs.hbr.org/2013/01/good-news-poor-leaders-can-cha/.

5. Tan, Chade-Meng. *Search Inside Yourself: The Unexpected Path to Achieving Success, Happiness (and World Peace)*. (New York: HarperOne, 2012), 163.

6. Cameron, Kim. *Positive Leadership: Strategies for Extraordinary Performance*. (San Francisco: Berrett-Koehler, 2012), 97.

7. Zenger, Jack and Joseph Folkman. "Are You Sure You're Not a Bad Leader?" *Harvard Business Review*. August 16, 2012. http://blogs.hbr.org/cs/2012/08/are_you_sure_youre_not_a_bad_b.html.

8. Achor, Shawn. "What Giving Gets You at the Office." *Harvard Business Review*. July 2011. http://blogs.hbr.org/2011/07/what-giving-gets-you-at-the-of/.

9. Fredrickson, Barbara. *Positivity: Groundbreaking Research Reveals How to Embrace the Hidden Strength of Positive Emotions, Overcome Negativity, and Thrive*. (New York: Crown Publishers, 2009), 167.

10. Goleman, Daniel. "When You Criticize Someone, You Make It Harder for that Person to Change." http://blogs.hbr.org/2013/12/when-you-criticize-someone-you-make-it-harder-for-them-to-change/.

11. Quinn, Ryan W. and Robert E. Quinn. *Lift: Becoming a Positive Force in Any Situation.* (San Francisco: Berrett-Koehler, 2009), 25.

12. Cameron, Kim. *Positive Leadership: Strategies for Extraordinary Performance,*19.

Chapter Four—Leadership Principle #3: Earn Credibility

1. Kouzes, Jim and Barry Posner. *Credibility: How Leaders Gain and Lose It, Why People Demand It.* (San Francisco: Jossey-Bass, 2011), 35.

2. Tan, Chade-Meng. *Search Inside Yourself: The Unexpected Path to Achieving Success, Happiness (and World Peace).* (New York: HarperOne, 2012), 176.

3. Ibid.

4. Fredrickson, *Positivity: Groundbreaking Research*, 180.

5. Kouzes, *Credibility: How Leaders Gain and Lose It, Why People Demand It*, 179.

6. Gruenfeld, Deborah and Zander, Lauren; "Authentic Leadership Can Be Bad Leadership." *Harvard Business Review.* February 2011.

5. Kouzes, *Credibility: How Leaders Gain and Lose It, Why People Demand It*, 179.

7. Goldsmith, Marshall. "The Success Delusion." *Conference Board Review.* January–February 2007. http://www.marshallgoldsmithlibrary.com/cim/articles_display.php?aid=321.

8. Sutton, Robert. "Why Good Bosses Tune in to Their People." *Forbes.* August 31, 2010.

9. Quinn, *Lift: Becoming a Positive Force in Any Situation,* 107.

10. Kouzes, *Credibility: How Leaders Gain and Lose It, Why People Demand It,* 199.

Chapter Five—Leadership Principle #4: Cultivate Compassion

1. Cuddy, Amy J.C., Matthew Kohut, and John Neffinger. "Connect, Then Lead." *Harvard Business Review.* July–August 2013.

2. Mutzabaugh, Ben. "Southwest Pilot Holds Flight for Grieving Grandfather." *USA Today.* January 11, 2011. http://travel. usatoday.com/flights/post/2011/01/southwest-pilot-holds-flight-for-grieving-grandfather/138762/1.

3. Lilius, Jacoba M., Monica C. Worline, Jane E. Dutton, Jason Kanov, Peter J. Frost, and Sally Maitlis. "What Good Is Compassion at Work?" Paper presented at the Academy of Management Meetings. August 1–6, 2003.

4. Cuddy, "Connect, Then Lead."

5. Loewenstein, George. "The Psychology of Curiosity: A Review and Reinterpretation." *Psychological Bulletin.* 1994;116(1):75–98.

6. Quinn, *Lift: Becoming a Positive Force in Any Situation.*

7. Loewenstein, "The Psychology of Curiosity: A Review and Reinterpretation," 75–98.

ACKNOWLEDGMENTS

S. Max Brown

This book is a reflection of conversations with people from all around the world. Each presentation, question, discussion, brainstorming session, break-time chat, radio show interview, book, article, or blog post helped to inform what is contained here. While my name is on the cover, I acknowledge the contributions of so many friends who have made this book a reality. Indeed, if I have ever done anything right, it is in engaging the right people who make me better every single day.

This project really started in 2007 after a presentation I made at a GE global engagement conference. Shortly thereafter, I found myself traveling to multiple sites working with GE leaders, and ultimately invited to be a regular presenter at their highest-rated leadership course. To do this, new content was required that was relevant, meaningful, and current. *Leadership Vertigo* was created as a result. While I strive to continually improve the product, I thank my friends at GE, including Mark, Tom, Bob, Kris, Fred, and the hundreds of participants in those leadership courses who have encouraged me the entire way.

In order for this to work, I needed time to create, build, and reflect. It was Peter Hart who made this possible. I'll never forget the day we spent talking about this book during a bus ride in Paris, France. Peter, your generosity of spirit and abundant mentality has enabled this to happen. Thank you.

Rideau's Real Recogniton Radio became a wonderful testing ground to engage global leaders in thoughtful conversations on how to help people thrive. Indeed, those conversations have found their way into this book in many places. I'm grateful to my co-host, Roy Saunderson, who helped push me to think through many of the concepts in a more thoughtful way.

I'm grateful to work and spend time with amazing leaders around the world. Leaders like Vineet Nayar, Doug Conant, Billy Taylor, Whitney Johnson, John Hope Bryant, Chade-Meng Tan, Jim Kouzes, Barbara Fredrickson, John Loomis, Brene Brown, Rich Fernandez, Clay Christensen, Kim Cameron, Adam Grant, Monica Diaz, Jim Kouzes, Gary Kelly, Mark Oakes, Lolly Daskal, Clark Campbell, Sean Gardner, Steve Keating, Anne Kreamer, Tony Meloto, Bruno Wierzbicki, Jamie Naughton, Mike Henry Sr., Mollie Marti, Dave Carpenter, Mike Myatt, Peter Block, Annette Simmons, Tonda Ferguson, and many others have influenced me through their words and their actions.

Still, no book can be written without words on paper, and I'm grateful that in 2010 I was able to find a writing partner who is skilled at his craft. Tanveer and I have worked countless mornings, nights, weekends, and holidays in order to put this together. It has not been easy, and the sacrifice to family and other priorities cannot be overstated. I'm grateful for his endurance, patience, and flexibility.

Finally, this leads to my wife, Sally, and my two amazing kids, AnLi and Drew. For years, they have patiently endured my travel schedule and the long weeks away from home, and the hours of reviews, drafts, and conference calls when I was home. Thank you for your feedback, encouragement, love, and support through it all.

I have inevitably forgotten to mention so many, and for this, I apologize. I simply express gratitude to all of you. I'm humbled to be surrounded by so many great people—grateful to call you my friends.

Tanveer Naseer

When you sit down to write a book, one thing that immediately becomes clear is that it's anything but a solo endeavor. In many ways, a book is a reflection not just of the experiences and insights of the writer, but of those around them who help to guide and shape the ideas that form the basis of their message.

As such, I would like to start off by thanking Doug Conant for taking the time to sit down with me to share his insights and experiences on leadership, as well as some personal stories of the impact his actions had on his employees, his family, and himself. Having the opportunity to discuss with him what he's found to be the necessary elements to successfully leading today's organizations proved invaluable in helping to articulate some of the ideas discussed in our chapter on the leadership principle Build Community.

In addition to Doug, I would also like to thank the following guests from my leadership show, "Leadership Biz Cafe": Guy Kawasaki, Teresa Amabile, Steven Kramer, Jesse Lynn Stoner, Dave Balter, Marlene Chism, Andrea Kates, Joel Garfinkle, Shama Kabani, Shirzad Chamine, Liz Wiseman, Erika Andersen, and Doug Lipp, whose conversations on leadership and the challenges we face in today's organizations have helped to elucidate and inform some of the ideas and thoughts that are shared in this book.

My thanks also go out to Matthew E. May, Liz Wiseman, and Carolyn Monaco, who graciously shared with me both their experiences and knowledge about the book writing and publishing experience, as well as some well-timed advice about some of the challenges to be found in the latter stages of publishing a book.

There are so many people who have been supportive and enthusiastic about my writings and work on leadership over the last several years and while I wish I could thank you all in these pages, I do want to extend a special note of thanks to Deb Mills-Scofield, Lolly Daskal, Jim Kouzes, Skip Pritchard, Meghan M. Biro, and Mike Myatt. Each of you has helped me to appreciate the value of my insights and writings. I'm truly grateful for your continued support and enthusiasm for my insights and ideas on leadership, as well as for your generosity of spirit and kindness in giving.

When writing a leadership book or blog, or even hosting a leadership show, it's not always easy to know what others are interested in learning more about, or what message will motivate them to become a better leader for their team and organization. And that's why I'd like to thank the loyal readers of my award-winning leadership blog on my website, TanveerNaseer. com. Thanks to you, I had an outlet to test and share some of the insights I've written about in this book—some of which you may recognize from the various breadcrumbs I sprinkled in my blog posts as a little peek of what I had in mind in writing this book. Your support and enthusiasm for my insights and writings on leadership served to fuel my drive to sit down and write my first leadership book. I look forward continuing to share my insights with you in preparation towards writing my next one.

And speaking of writing, I'd like to express my gratitude to my cowriter for this book, S. Max Brown, for joining me on this journey of writing this book. We've had many thought-provoking and exciting conversations about the future of leadership, and what our own experiences and insights reveal as the opportunities to be found in these new, unchartered waters. Although we came into this project from different vantage points, it was clear right from the start that we had a common message we wanted to share about how we can help leaders not just do better, but be the better version of themselves. It's been quite the adventure, my friend.

Of course, no acknowledgment in this book could be complete without expressing my heartfelt gratitude and love to my wife, Andrée, not only for her willingness to read and re-read our manuscript as it underwent the various additions/revisions to get it to a completed stage, but also for her endless support and encouragement as this book transformed over the years from a mere concept to the completed book you now hold in your hands. Andrée, this book is as much your accomplishment as it is mine. Thank you for always believing in me and for willingly taking my hand to join me on this crazy ride.

And speaking of crazy rides, I also want to thank my three daughters—Alya, Malaika, and Zafina—for being so understanding about how much time and effort was required in making this book a reality. All three of you have shown such maturity in your understanding and patience as this project took more of my time as it evolved, changed, and grew. Your support, love, and encouragement gave me the strength and motivation to keep pushing ahead regardless of what stood before me. I sincerely hope through my example you've been inspired to see how you can achieve the dreams you hold dear if you're willing to believe in yourself and take that leap of faith forward.

ABOUT THE
AUTHORS

S. Max Brown

@SMaxBrown

Max is the VP of Leadership & Culture at Pluralsight, a senior advisor to the Shingo Institute at Utah State University, and a thought leader in motivation and organizational behavior.

Over the past twenty years, Max has made over two thousand presentations and met with leaders in locations all around the world. He's taken clients rappelling off the Great Wall of China, facilitated at the Parliament of World Religions Conference in Spain, and spoken in hundreds of cities including Athens, Bangalore, Beijing, Dublin, Hong Kong, The Hague, Mumbai, Paris, New York, Shanghai, Singapore, Toronto, Vancouver, and Sydney . . . Nebraska.

Max regularly presents at one of GE's highest-rated leadership programs. He is a recommended "all-star" keynote speaker from the International Association of Business Communicators and his keynotes consistently receive rave reviews from clients like 3M, American Express, Southwest Airlines, The Nature Conservancy, HSBC, and The Canadian Federal Government. He has a certificate in Leadership Coaching from Georgetown University, a master's degree in Organizational Learning from George Mason University, and graduated magna cum laude from Brigham Young University. He also speaks Mandarin Chinese after seven years of living in Taipei and Shanghai.

Max and his wife, Sally, live in Salt Lake City, Utah and they are the proud parents of two amazing kids. When they have time, they love spending time on their ranch in Idaho.

Previous adventures include coaching clients and building a retail business in China, co-hosting the Real Recognition Radio show, shark diving off the coast of Honduras, and horse riding in Inner Mongolia.

Tanveer Naseer

@TanveerNaseer

Tanveer Naseer is an award-winning and internationally-acclaimed leadership writer and speaker. He is also the Principal and Founder of Tanveer Naseer Leadership, a leadership coaching firm that works with executives and managers to help them develop practical leadership and team-building competencies to guide organizational growth and development.

Tanveer credits his background and experiences in the scientific field for his keen understanding of the nature of interactions in business, as well as being able to help organizations break down and improve complex processes which are holding their teams back.

Tanveer's writings and insights on leadership and workplace interactions have been featured in a number of prominent organization and media publications, including *Fast Company*, American Management Association, SmartBrief, Canada's national newspaper *The Globe and Mail*, Human Capital Institute, CAREEREALISM, Hallmark Business Connections, and numerous industry trade publications and newsletters.

Tanveer's writings have also been recommended by The Governor General of Canada's Canadian Leadership Conference.

Tanveer is the recipient of several awards and recognitions as one of today's leading and influential thinkers in the leadership sphere, including being recognized by *Inc. Magazine* as one of the Top 100 Leadership and Management Experts, ranking #3 on HR Examiner's Top 25 Online Influencers in Leadership, as well as being featured on numerous lists as one of the top leadership writers in the world.

For the past three years, Tanveer has also served as the chairman of the governing board for one of the largest regional high schools in the province of Quebec, Canada.

Tanveer holds a Master of Science degree in Pathology from McGill University and currently lives in Montreal, Canada, with his wife, Andrée, and their three daughters.

To learn more about Tanveer's work and his writings on leadership, visit his website: TanveerNaseer.com.

ABOUT FAMILIUS

Welcome to a place where books—and family—are beautiful. Familius: a book publisher dedicated to helping families be happy.

Visit Our Website: www.familius.com

Our website is a different kind of place. Get inspired, read articles, discover books, watch videos, connect with our family experts, download books and apps and audiobooks, and along the way, discover how values and happy family life go together.

Join Our Family

There are lots of ways to connect with us! Subscribe to our newsletters at www.familius.com to receive uplifting inspiration, essays from our Pater Familius, a free ebook every month, and the first word on special discounts and Familius news.

Become an Expert

Familius authors and other established writers interested in helping families be happy are invited to join our family and contribute online content. If you have something important to say on the family, join our expert community by applying at:

www.familius.com/apply-to-become-a-familius-expert

Get Bulk Discounts

If you feel a few friends and family might benefit from what you've read, let us know and we'll be happy to provide you with quantity discounts. Simply email us at specialorders@familius.com.

Website: www.familius.com
Facebook: www.facebook.com/paterfamilius
Twitter: @familiustalk, @paterfamilius1
Pinterest: www.pinterest.com/familius

 The most important work you ever do will be within the walls of your own home.

NOTES

NOTES

NOTES

NOTES

NOTES

NOTES